how i learned to snap

learned to snap

Kirk
Read

A Small-Town
Coming-Out
and
Coming-of-Age
Story

d

Hill Street Press
Athens, Georgia

A HILL STREET PRESS BOOK

Published in the United States of America by
Hill Street Press LLC
191 East Broad Street, Suite 209
Athens, Georgia 30601-2848 USA
706-613-7200
info@hillstreetpress.com
www.hillstreetpress.com

Hill Street Press is committed to preserving the written word. Every effort is made to print
books on acid-free paper with a significant amount of post-consumer recycled content.

Jacket and text design by Anne Richmond Boston.
All photographs courtesy of the author.

Printed in the United States of America.

Library of Congress Cataloging-in-Publication Data

Read, Kirk, 1973–
        How I Learned to Snap : a Southern coming-out and coming-of-age story / by Kirk
Read.
                p.   cm.
        ISBN 1-58818-039-5 (acid-free paper)
        1. Read, Kirk, 1973- 2. Gay high school students—Virginia—Lexington—Biography.
        3. Gay teenagers—Virginia—Lexington—Biography. 4. Coming out (Sexual orienta
        tion)—Virginia—Lexington. I. Title

        HQ75.8.R4 A3 2001
        305.235—dc21   2001016860

ISBN # 1-58818-039-5

10 9 8 7 6 5 4 3 2 1

First printing

for Richard Labonté

con

tents

prologue

Lake County, California, is a lumpy casserole of good country people, leftover hippies, and hardcore druggies. The speed problem
here has prompted Senator Barbara Boxer to urge a ten-mil-
lion-dollar "clean-up" of its meth labs, many of which are situ-
ated in Clearlake garages. You haven't lived until you've bowled
next to a pack of rednecks on homemade speed. Their prison
tattoos and dirty fingernails make me wonder what in the world
I'm doing here, why I don't sleep with a gun under my pillow, and
why, of all places, I came here to write a book about being openly
gay in high school.

The week I traded San Francisco for Lake County, I got a tarot
reading from an old-school gay hippie who makes his living
from tie-dye. I've historically dismissed tarot readings as the
New Age equivalent of kids at a slumber party huddled around
a Ouija board, but I thought it would be good trashy fun, and
in a county where Wal-Mart and K-Mart are the cultural epi-
centers, a bit of camp is always welcome.

The tarot queen said there would be a sign. I envisioned earthquakes, floods, and the reawakening of the supposedly dormant
Mount Konocti volcano, the imposing stature of which fills the
window of my writing studio. "You'll know it when you see it," he
assured me.

My sign came in the form of a teenage boy. I'm leery of the
word *boy* being applied to teenagers. The word is so often used in

the media to portray teenage sex as criminal and horrific. Once you've traded Legos for masturbation, you're not really a boy anymore, are you? But this young man, around fifteen, was undeniably a delicate, peachfuzzy boy.

The ambitiously named Café at Wal-Mart was bustling at lunchtime. I was feeling appropriately guilty about my burger and fries, and even worse about spending money at a corporate chain that feeds so much cash to right-wing crazies. This was an East coast lapse in scruples, to be sure.

Amidst those lunching at tiny Formica tables, the boy sat with his mother. He sported a ponytail tied off with a purple scrunchie. His well-conditioned hair hung over the left shoulder of his Calvin Klein tee shirt. I don't think he wanted that ponytail out of his sight, because he kept petting the end of it as if it were a hamster. His fingers were covered with silver rings and he ate quickly, as if some coyote were poised to leap atop the table and finish his tater tots for him. His mother was a round woman dressed in an embroidered Guatemalan shirt I'd seen priced three for a dollar at the Hospice Thrift Shop. He was chubby from sharing his mother's snacks. I wondered how long it would take him to reach her size.

They spoke without looking at one another. I sat at the table behind his mother, catching pieces of their quiet conversation. Names like *Pa* and *Aunt Junebug* floated over to me. The boy saw my tee shirt—two baby girls kissing. He looked up from his food to throw glances at me. As he lifted his burger, his pinkies jutted out from the sides of the bun. He was a dainty eater and wiped the sides of his mouth with a small stack of napkins after each bite.

He looked at me again, this time longer. I turned my head so he could get a good look without feeling so self-conscious. When I returned his stare, our eyes locked. I was careful, aware that this was not my turf. In the Castro or Chelsea, such looks are part of the cultural fabric. But I was home again, back in the land of nervous gestures and crude guesswork as to the substance of a stranger's gaze.

I went through high school dreaming of being rescued by an as-yet-undiscovered older brother who would adopt me and ask why I looked so sad. I stared at older men I thought might be candidates and was thoroughly heartbroken every time the connection didn't occur the way I'd written it in my journal.

His eyes were full of a need for adoption. I wasn't cruising him. I was gently, carefully letting him know that his tribe was out there, beyond the cinderblocks and hubcaps that filled his front yard. It took me ten years to make it to the other side of this dynamic. How many strangers had I set my eyes upon, begging for reassurance? In that moment, I wished I could have handed him something useful—something more than a smile, something more than a soft-eyed stare that said "hang in there" or "save your money."

The curtain opened slowly. Ian Halsted had just finished a spot-on piano rendition of Dave Brubeck's "Take Five." It drew polite applause. The gymnasium of Lylburn Downing Middle School was completely dark. When the curtain was drawn, the lights came up on Jesse Fowler, who was standing center stage with his back to the audience. The ominous, pounding strains of Michael Jackson's "Beat It" erupted from the speakers. With each chord, Jesse raised an arm above his head, alternating left and right, just like Michael in the video.

When the drumbeats gently entered the mix, Jesse threw his arms to the side and added his torso to the dance. The guitar roared in, and Jesse spun around on the ball of his right foot. The audience screamed. He was wearing mirrored sunglasses and the kind of red, heavily zippered jacket that Michael Jackson had just introduced to the world. Where had Jesse gotten it? Where had a white boy learned to dance like that?

The black girls were standing by this point, waving their hands in the air. The rest of the audience sat, slackjawed, beholding the purely alien being before them. During Eddie Van Halen's guitar solo, Jesse whipped off his sunglasses and tossed them to the side of the stage. He shuffled his feet, copping moves from the video he'd no doubt watched hundreds of times. But this was more than karaoke footwork. Jesse took ample inspiration, but made the song completely his own.

I was in fourth grade at the time, 1983, sitting on the front row with a broken ankle. Jesse was in seventh grade. His thirteen years made him Moses-size to me. Halfway through the song, Mason Emore leaned over to me and said, "He's a faggot." I cringed, knowing what a horrible thing that must be.

I couldn't take my eyes away from him. Neither could anyone else. Tasha Nelson was dancing in the aisle like she was at a tent revival. Every move Jesse made drew a collective roar. The black girls had moved up to the front and were spinning furiously, six feet beneath his gyrating body. Jesse worked his way across the entire stage, shedding his jacket to reveal a white tee shirt and blue jeans.

Now he was at the part where the gangs do battle in the video. As he shook and kicked, I saw fifty dancers in his wake, preparing to kill one another. The lyric "They'll kick you and they'll beat you and they'll tell you it's fair" would come back to haunt Jesse, but for now, he was Michael Jackson, the gang peacemaker. He was the skinny little white town faggot who, for four minutes, was being worshiped by five hundred people.

The audience starting clapping a full minute before the song was over, and as the music faded, Jesse vanished stage left. He would not grant them the satisfaction of a bow. He disappeared as completely as he had materialized.

The floor of the gym was vibrating with stomping feet. I stood, leaning on my crutches, and jumped up and down on one foot.

"He's got it in the bag," said a girl who was dressed up for a skit that was yet to come. She said it with awe, not jealousy.

As the cheering subsided, I heard people murmuring about Jesse being a faggot, but they were still clapping. I didn't really know what a faggot was, except that Jesse must be one. Faggots, it seemed, got huge applause.

The other acts included a group lip-synch to the country tune "Swingin'" with a full set that included a kitchenette, a porch swing, and a sofa barely fit for the front yard. Several people sang, danced, or did send-up skits of their favorite teachers. But, after Jesse, they all looked like firefighters digging around the rubble of a gutted homestead.

Jesse won. It was my first taste of real justice and my introduction to the boy who would change my life forever.

The next morning, I saw Jesse walking across the street from school. He was flanked by four girls and was dressed in a white oxford shirt and khaki pants. His expressive lisp poked out of the protective tent his girlfriends created around him. Every time he spoke, the girls tittered and squealed with laughter. He clutched his books to his chest just like they did. Even I knew that was a no-no.

I planted my crutches under my arms and walked toward them. My ankle had shattered when I was thrown from a pony named Goldie. I still hadn't gotten the hang of my crutches but crossed the schoolyard as quickly as I could. I was almost there, imagining what I would say to him. Maybe I would compliment him on his dance. Maybe I would ask if I could come over to his house. Maybe I would just say hello.

Jesse and his entourage noisily progressed across the schoolyard. Everyone watched him pass, like some sort of leper messiah. As he and the girls bounded into the front door of the gym, I knew I wasn't going to catch up. It would be a long time before I was able to move that quickly.

Camp

Indubitably, there were attempts made during my childhood to ensure that all hands were on deck in the matter of young Kirk's masculine development. At age ten I was sent to a boy's camp in southwest Virginia. The whole thing was rather unseemly. The accommodations, for one thing, lacked a certain dignity. This meant bunking with seven boys, one junior counselor named Porky, and two counselors for whom I harbored enormous crushes. They were mostly patient with me, concerned enough, and had adult penises, the likes of which I'd never seen. This was an early lesson in what corporate trainers call "the trade-off."

We had to wear black mesh tank tops with orange lettering that read *Camp Commonwealth* in an antique stencil font. I was forced to engage in archery and spent afternoons at the rifle range. The closest thing to an arts-and-crafts period was a woodshop, where I painstakingly built, sanded, and stained a bookshelf for my mother. The best part of woodshop was that a crazy older boy was in charge. He'd play Clash and Ramones albums and encourage us all to learn the words so we could sing along. "Beat on the Brat" was a favorite. I took stylistic notes that would later enable me to escape the heavy metal haze of junior high school. Better to listen to ten-year-old punk, than to spend junior high sneaking joints in my parents' basement, listening to Black Sabbath. One is never too young to develop standards.

Just outside the woodshop was a baseball diamond. Junior campers gathered around the chain link fence behind the batter's box to watch the older guys play. I'd only played softball in P.E. class, with a mixture of boys and girls. We pitched underhand and never slid into base unless we were serving up drama. These boys, however, were hell-bent on keeping that ball moving as fast as possible. I could see their pupils dilate with boy-rage as they spat. I wanted no part of this little activity period. I lacked the coordination and warrior training that would have made such a game remotely bearable.

My first week at camp, I fell off a horse and sprained my wrist. I'd already broken an ankle and had nearly broken my buttbone riding horses, so I was irritated that I was expected to ride at all, having retired a year earlier.

"Back up on," the barn manager said. "Back up on."

That's when I started crying manufactured but wet and noisy tears, hoping that this barn Nazi would cut the platitudes and take me to the infirmary. I knew Mrs. Gardener would call my parents, who would take me to the hospital and see what an egregious error had been made in sending me to camp at all.

Hmmm . . . let's do the math: a creative, empathic child with lots of girls for friends at a six-week athletic camp for boys. This was a rare lapse in parenting for Mom and Dad, whose laissez-faire discipline was close to pitch perfect.

I don't blame my parents Suzanne and Bev here. Their advisors had been the Murphies, whose son was a smelly-armpitted all-American B-O-Y who did not harbor crushes on Jim Palmer and Burt Reynolds. My parents were highly suggestible, and I'm sure that my father, who'd earned the rank of U.S. Army colonel, saw in me the end of three generations of Read men at the Virginia Military Institute. He panicked. They shipped me off to camp.

My mother did make a nod to my creative side, bless her. She lined my trunk with checkerboard shelf paper and together we filled in the blank squares with black Magik Markers. Not all of them, mind you, but a symmetrical *pattern* of them. It was the first time I remember being awestruck by my mother.

My parents retrieved me from camp the very afternoon I sprained my wrist and took me to a doctor in Lexington. One perk of my trip home was that I got to see *Pirates of Penzance* at Henry Street Playhouse, the local community theater. I wanted to be on that stage, wearing tights and snuggling in the laps of burly pirates. I wanted to be Shirley Temple, not Knute Rockney. I cried the entire way back to camp, hoping for a reprieve. As my parents dropped me off, Dad told me to "suck it up." I had five weeks left, and I was on my own. This called for drastic measures, my first foray into petty crime.

My first night back, with the camp's proprietors in the kitchen after dinner, I snuck out of the dining hall and opened a window in the main office. I crawled in and opened "The Book," which was the master schedule of boys, their activities, and, I would later learn, their medical peculiarities.

My handwriting was still very childish. I didn't take to cursive at all and promptly forgot it after third grade. All of the entries here were in Mrs. Gardener's tight, efficient script. I didn't want to risk apprehension, so I studied the book's entries. I noticed that some boys had double periods of certain activities. This was designated by a single arrow through the gridded column. I feverishly erased my baseball period as well as my horseback period, giving myself a triple period in the woodshop—five weeks of punk and wood.

I looked at my afternoon activities: tennis, soccer, archery, and the highly dreaded rifle range. Did my parents know their ten-year-old was shooting guns? Who thought that was a good idea? Soccer was the most palatable item on Camp Commonwealth's athletic agenda. I'd been playing since I could walk, thanks to my older brother Hunter. As soon as the diapers came off, Hunter set up cones in the backyard and put me through rigorous dribbling exercises. My neighbors Kent and Sammy turned their family playroom into a makeshift indoor soccer arena, much to the chagrin of their mother. The three of us broke windows and stained the walls with blood smears. But I learned to love soccer.

As for the rest of my Boy 101 classes, I knew I'd just have to endure those afternoons. A full day in the woodshop would get me caught for sure. The last thing I needed was Mrs. Gardener showing up at the woodshop, taking me by the hand and explaining that I needed to "branch out in my interests."

Once my wrist healed, I again fell prey to the physical torments of prepubescent boys. The homophobic slurs and fagbaiting never slowed down during my injury, but now I was fair game for fights. To everyone's surprise, I held my own during most of these skirmishes. The boys in my cabin were mostly little Richmond brats from Collegiate, an upper-crust day school that parents loved to pretend was Eton. I hated every one of those pasty-faced little fuckers, especially the ones in my cabin. The Blackhawk cabin, as we were called.

Rudy, a Mohawk from next door, was particularly relentless. "Faggot," "little bitch," and "butt pirate" were some of his favorites epithets for me. He was a solid, tall boy, and probably had twenty pounds on me. So most nights I just let him jab at me as I made my way to the outhouse. (Yes, we used an outhouse.) As I brushed my teeth, he'd stab me with the end of his toothbrush. The counselors did nothing about it, subscribing to the same Darwinesque theory I encountered at school: "Boys will be boys who will help other boys be better boys."

One afternoon, returning to Blackhawk cabin from the rifle range, I was struck with a bout of homesickness. This was a near-daily occurrence for me.

Rudy sidled up to me with his broom. He was carrying it as part of a secret society initiation. I was never tapped for this dubious honor. Boys who were selected had to carry a broom for a week so they could sweep on demand. The boys endured more taunts than usual, and were required to do push-ups and give impromptu recitations of insipid camp poems. Given my crocodile tears, athletic avoidance, and regal demeanor, I was hardly secret society material.

Rudy dropped two steps behind me and put the broom handle against my butt. He pushed.

"Want a wedgie, faggot?"

I knew that unleashing my already considerable repertoire of snappy retorts would only result in further abuse, so I said nothing. Rudy persisted, smacking my ass with the straw end of the broom. I calmly brushed the dirt and lint from my shorts.

"Aw, is the faggot dirty? Is that little pussy-ass dirty?"

Had we been twenty years older, this kind of talk might have turned me on. I was terrified of him, but I also wondered where he'd found such marvelous words.

We stepped onto the cabin's porch and he followed me inside. We were alone. When he could see that he wasn't going to get a rise out of me, he hit me with the wooden handle. He missed my ass altogether. The wooden handle smacked my thighs hard enough to sting. I freaked.

I may not have been the strongest kid, but I'd been playing soccer for enough years that I had big legs. I kicked him in the stomach as hard as I could. He doubled over and let out a decidedly girlish moan. Inspired by far too much pro wrestling, I continued my assault.

He stirred, and I took a few hits to my gut. They only made me angrier. He was a lot bigger than I was and managed to flip me over and pin me down on the wooden floor. He held my face with one hand and spat in my eye.

"Fuckin' queer faggot."

A crowd was gathering on the porch. Four or five boys were on tiptoe, looking through the screen windows.

I don't think any of us fully realized that these words referred to a type of man who likes other men. They were mostly epithets for weakness. For all their venom, these nasty children weren't very inventive with their slurs.

"Get him, Rudy," they screamed. People always cheer for the winner. In this case, Rudy was the obvious winner. It was almost uninteresting, actually. He was much bigger and he was on top of me punching me in the stomach. This fight probably wasn't going to yield any change-up drama.

That was when all the boys started screaming "faggot" and "get him." I started struggling, beginning to panic about how much Rudy was going to hurt me. I broke free of him and scooted onto the junior counselor's bed. If I was going to get pounded, at least a bed would be more comfortable than the floor.

We tussled, and I knocked his head straight back against the wall. The thud, coupled with the continued screams of our growing audience, gave me an adrenalin rush like I'd never experienced. Was *this* why boys play baseball?

I rolled on top of Rudy and punched him square in the face for the first time. As my fist connected with his chin, I could feel my knuckles spraining. But it felt amazing. Rudy let out a groan and the boys on the porch started to cheer for me.

"Get him, Kirk. *Get him.*"

I used the blunt heels of my fists, opposite my thumbs, to beat on his chest and face. I knew I was hitting like a girl but I didn't care. This way, I'd last longer. Rudy curled up and fought back less. Occasionally he'd reach up to pop me on the chin. Boys love hitting each other in the face. I guess it's the next best thing to a kiss.

The boys on the porch were stomping and banging their fists on the shutters. The cabin shook. They were cheering for me. All these boys who'd called me "faggot" were calling my name and yelling for me to beat the hell out of the brat who'd made my life miserable.

I felt a head rush and a surge of hormones, like I'd shot up with steroids. I grabbed the edge of the mattress and pulled as hard as I could. I pulled the plastic handles so hard that one of them ripped. Rudy rolled face down onto the metal bedsprings. I threw the mattress on top of him and climbed on. I punched the mattress with full-knuckle fists and plunged my knees into him. He started screaming hysterically and I wondered whether I could really hurt him now.

The boys on the porch stopped their stomping and fell silent. I heard Scott, one of our counselors, screaming "Hey, what's going on?" from outside the cabin.

I stood up on the bed and jumped up and down on Rudy.

"Who's the faggot? Who's the faggot? Who's the faggot?" I screamed.

Scott pulled me off the bed with the decisive sweep of a single arm. The boys rushed in and lifted the mattress off Rudy, who was curled up in a fetal position. He was quivering, trying to hide his tears. We all just stood around him. No one knew what to say.

I spent the rest of the week at the woodshop. No one came to get me or said a word about the incident for the remainder of camp. Rudy started being nice to me. Now we had something in common. The other bullies left me alone after that.

Camp Commonwealth was intended as a kind of Final Solution for my sissy spirit, but I never told my parents about the fight. I wonder if Dad would have been proud that I'd won.

class of '95

As was true for many Virginia Military Institute men, Dad's priorities were VMI, the Army, God, and Family—in that order. He was the editor of the alumni publication, although an assistant did the actual editing while he kept in touch with hundreds of alumni. Dad shook a lot of hands. The world, to him, was a giant cocktail party, a room to be worked. I've never seen anyone who could talk to so many people and actually maintain a sense of sincerity. The VMI job was perfect for him, because it meant that my family's life was a continuous blur of cocktail parties, banquets, and luncheons.

"Class of '95" was the phrase Dad used to introduce me to his friends, often before my name was even uttered. It sounded to me like a particularly vulgar epithet. I grew up with a framed provisional appointment on my wall. This meant that when I was sixteen, I'd have a sit-down with VMI's dean of admissions to discuss my future as a VMI man.

Whenever I got angry with my father, I tossed the appointment down the steps, often followed by Norman Vincent Peale's *The Story of Jesus* and the weighty *Young Reader's Bible*. It was so gratifying to see the Colonel's sacred totems, manhood and God, bouncing down the steps like dropped boxes. After replacing the glass on that damn appointment three times, my mother suggested that it become an archival piece in my baby trunk.

Our household was military, to be sure, but I never employed the words *sir* or *ma'am* unless I was trying to curry favor with friends of my parents who were orthodox Army. Dad didn't do the Great Santini with me. He was fifty-three when I was born, eighteen years older than my mother. I think he'd gotten most of that out of his system with my five older siblings. We had our moments of struggle, as is to be expected, but Mom had taught me that in a pinch, bitch trumps bastard. As it became apparent that I was an extremely willful child, my father knew he was outnumbered by bitches.

By the time I was eleven, Dad had pretty much accepted that the Read family's venerated tradition at Virginia Military Institute was over. Certain moments jump to mind as early indicators. Every May Day, our gym class would rehearse a group dance to such classics as "Rock Around the Clock" and Abba's "Super Trouper." Once, when the living room was full of my father's crankiest army buddies, two martinis south, I appeared, boom box in hand to revive my performance. I was spunky, like I was auditioning for *Annie*. During the course of my three-and-a-half minute dance recital, everyone in the room finished their drinks.

Another time, my niece was at our house. My father was in the front hallway, rifling through one of the many piles of papers on his desk. I said to her, "Watch this." I cranked Madonna's "Like a Virgin" and descended the staircase, singing, humping the banister, and generally making my father apoplectic. Watching him squirm was one of my favorite things in the world. The Colonel was so entertaining when he was indignant.

Shortly thereafter, my father sat me down. One of my brothers had recently broken rank and gone to a state school that was notably *not* VMI. "Son," he said, "it looks like your brother isn't cut out for VMI. In your case, I don't think VMI's cut out for you. Go wherever you want." That said, I was free to plan a future free of push-ups, dreadful diarrhea-green outfits, and cue ball hairstyles.

This was before talk shows featured out-of-control children being sent to boot camp. (I probably would have fallen in love with the drill sergeant anyway, and left daisies on his pillow.) Besides, I got good grades and behaved well enough for my father to retire his riding crop. Being a tough disciplinarian with five children had worn him out. The older boys in my family got punched, and the girls got grounded. Me, I was assigned to write essays.

My father never spanked me, which is probably why today nothing hits the spot like a good over-the-knee paddling. He never even grounded me. I guess being a hard-ass had taken its toll on my father after three wars and thirty years of active duty. He'd really mellowed.

Mom was a Welcome Wagon lady when they met in 1970. Dad was working at the Pentagon and had three children from the first of his three previous marriages. His first wife was said to have died of a barbiturate overdose, which was either an accident or a suicide, depending on which family member was telling the story. Mom was also a single parent, with two kids by her first husband, who had left her suddenly to "find himself" in California. It was kind of like the *Brady Bunch*, but directed by Robert Altman and with a script by Pat Conroy.

There was an eighteen-year gap between my parents, which concerned my father even though Dad always looked fifteen years younger than he was, with a baby face and a little help from Grecian Formula. Mom was totally unlike his previous wives, each of whom had fallen into more traditional categories of the Military Wife. Mom was a self-described "ample" woman with fiery brown eyes and an earthy yet regal demeanor. She'd grown up as a white-gloved D.C. debutante, playing touch football with the Kennedys and attending dancing school with Alfred Friendly.

Mom had a sensitive bullshit detector, though. At age nineteen, she crawled out the basement window of her snotty junior college dormitory and bought a one-way ticket to Reno. Amo, my maternal grandmother, took to her sickbed for dramatic effect and set up a wet bar in the hospital room. But her Suzanne never came home.

Dad tried to discourage Mom's pursuit of marriage by detailing the occasions during which he'd killed men in combat. She insisted that he was, deep down, a pushover. She nicknamed him The Ruthless Marshmallow. He told her he'd been one of the first Americans into Hiroshima after the bombing. He told her about highly classified underground nuclear testing projects he'd overseen. But hearing about top-secret government missions must have turned my mother on, because she wouldn't take no for an answer. Due to years of radiation exposure and high blood pressure, Dad wasn't expected to live past his sixtieth birthday. "I can only give you a few years," he told Mom.

They eloped a year after they met, to Amo's horror. She was an old-school socialite whose idea of heaven was a fat credit limit at Lord & Taylor, a glass of scotch, and a handful of Valium. She said that it would be a "tragedy" for my parents to have another child. Mom didn't blink, because Dad had her convinced that he was sterile from all that radiation. Mom was five months pregnant with me before she called her mother to say she was "having a little tragedy." Until that point, Mom thought I was a stomach tumor.

After Mom and Dad married, they left northern Virginia to live in Dad's hometown of Lexington, Virginia, where I was born in 1973. My five older siblings are anywhere between eleven and twenty-five years older than I am. Paige and Hunter, Mom's kids from her first marriage, were still in high school when I was a toddler, so I had a brief taste of life with older siblings. Dad's three kids were in their twenties by then, so they were more like cousins I saw only at Thanksgiving and Christmas. I grew up alongside their children and always had trouble explaining to classmates why one of my nieces was a year older than I was. "Your family is *confusing*," a friend told me in kindergarten.

When my mouth got me ejected from Vacation Bible School for blasphemy, which it did from time to time, Dad was there to assign me a series of essay questions. He'd make comments in the margins of my essay and we'd proceed to argue for hours on end. His father had been a professor of English and Dad had also taught English. I guess this seemed like punishment to him, but it was perfect for me I got to act up, justify it in print, and argue with the Colonel.

The worst argument we ever had was over the Holy Trinity when I was twelve. I can safely say it was the worst because much of it was spent with Dad pounding his fist on my great grandfather's dining room table as Mom watched with arms akimbo.

During Sunday school, I'd declared that the Holy Trinity was "bullshit." My beleaguered teacher gave me the rest of that Sunday morning off. I'd already started my essay before Dad got home, which I peppered with the word "bullshit." I argued that no one could give me a convincing explanation as to how three people could be one person at the same time.

I looked at my father and said, "It's like when you look up a word in the dictionary and it uses the same word in the definition. Like *bullshit* meaning 'the shit of a bull.' *It's bullshit.*" That's when Dad started pounding his fist on the table.

Several months later, I started confirmation class, which is what you do when you're twelve in the Methodist church. The very first day, our minister did chalk drawings of the Holy Trinity on the church classroom blackboard. I scowled as he explained the whole three-for-the-price-of-one-theory. I argued a little but not nearly enough to warrant an early exit. I sat back and played the game, knowing that it would kill Dad if I didn't receive a proper confirmation. That day, I learned about the tenuous relationship between saying what needs to be said and breaking my father's heart.

the yellow sweater

I'd had the same bowl-and-bangs haircut since I was old enough to toddle down to the barbershop where, invariably, I was treated to the hunting stories and racist diatribes of other customers. Dad got his hair cut once a week, while my mother visited the Glamour House once every other week. Whoever assumes vanity and fastidiousness are exclusively female qualities hasn't taken a good hard look at the grooming regimen of men who've done time in our nation's military.

When I was twelve, something clicked inside me. Perhaps it was my gay biological clock, perhaps it was the beginning of my rebellion. Or maybe I was simply tired of looking like a Little Rascal. For whatever reason, I announced to my mother that I wanted Danielle to cut my hair. The benefit of having an overcommitted, workaholic, save-the-world kind of father is that he is often oblivious to the minutiae of one's daily life.

I fantasized about this haircut for weeks, cutting and pasting hundreds of photographs from *GQ* and *Esquire* onto the walls of my bedroom. The whole mannish-boy thing was working my nerves. The spinning blue-and-red stripes of the barber's pole were about to be relegated to memory.

And not a moment too soon. I'd discovered the Smiths, Depeche Mode, and the Cure. I wanted to be free, if only in scalp. Doesn't freedom begin at the top and work its way down? It was 1985, the height of the Reagan era, so those trickle-down theories were ubiquitous.

I told anyone at school who would listen that I was going to have my hair "styled." Mostly I told girls, who understood such things. For good measure, I mentioned it to several of my guy friends, most of whom looked down at their shoes and said, "Uh, what does that mean?" I probably made it sound like I was going in for purple-and-gold extensions, when in actuality, all I wanted was a part and a bit of layering. The reception of my big hair news was good, with the exception of one girl.

During marching band practice, I'd confided in her the most important development of my life so far and she'd responded, "Are you a boy or a girl?"

I didn't slap Elsie. Instead, she slapped me. I called her a "fucking bitch" in front of her all-girl clique, the coterie in which I so desperately wanted membership. She gave me an anemic half-slap, then held her hand in the air as if it were bloody.

"I'm so sorry," she squeaked. "Did I hurt you?"

"You're gonna have to hit a lot harder if you want it to hurt," I coached her.

Mom was in many ways responsible for my growing interest in fashion. She'd taken the entire family to Mrs. Windsor, the Color Me Beautiful woman, where a dozen of us took turns being evaluated in her basement.

When Mrs. Windsor got me in that chair, she held swatches of color against my face, then told my family which ones worked.

"Kirk is a classic autumn," she said.

That explains *everything*, I thought.

She held purples and browns against me, saying "Oh, Kirk! Star!" if a color was especially compatible with my skin tones. At first I wasn't all that thrilled to be an autumn. It meant that I was stuck with, as my mother put it, "diarrhea green and doody brown." Mrs. Windsor reassured me that Ronald Reagan had made it okay for people to wear brown suits. This came as some relief.

She gave me a small plastic booklet of fabric swatches, which I took with me everywhere, like a prayer book. I told my mother that from that point forward, I would only wear season-appropriate colors. Furthermore, my church clothes had to go because Mrs. Windsor had forbidden me to wear white and blue shirts. "Cream," she cooed. "Oyster. *Beige.*" She made it sound illicit. I proceeded to break my friends into skin tone groupings—yellow and blue. I gave them advice on what to wear and even scolded teachers for wearing scarves that were all wrong for them.

"You're just making it worse," I said to my science teacher. "Trust me on this."

Shortly after the girls at the Glamour House styled my hair, Mom agreed to take me shopping at Valley View, the new mall in Roanoke. I mostly wanted to go into girl stores, like the Limited. I couldn't imagine why they didn't have men's clothes. Mom tried to steer me toward boy stores where I could get measured for khakis and oxford cloth shirts, but I was relentless.

In Chess King, I spotted it—a neon-yellow cotton knit sweater. It was the last one, so the clerk had to take it off the mannequin. I put it on and stood in front of my mother.

Mom tilted her head, then grimaced. "It's bright yellow," she said.

"Mom, it's my color. Look!" I held a swatch of lemon yellow against the sweater. The sweater was considerably brighter, but Mom bought it anyway. On the way home, I rhapsodized about the various outfits I could build around that sweater.

At school the next day, I rolled and unrolled the cuffs of my sweater while Mrs. Mears covered the chalkboard with detailed notes about study skills. We were learning how to make flashcards and she passed out index cards so we could practice. On my card, I made a list of various shirts that would work under the sweater, then considered wearing the sweater without a shirt—but only girls did that. I crossed through that idea with so many lines that no one would ever be able to read it.

Between classes, three boys followed me in the hallway, pulling on the hem of the sweater.

"Yellow sweater, yellow sweater!" they screamed. I brushed it off, leaning against the lockers of girlfriends who assured me, "It really *is* your color."

By the end of the day, the boys' teasing had gotten to me. After lunch, I'd left the sweater in my locker, hoping they would stop. The three boys had increased their ranks exponentially. By the time the final bell rang, upwards of twenty boys were poking at me, smacking the back of my head and stepping up their verbal assault to "yellow sweater faggot." Young homophobes are *so* creative.

Despite the cold, after school I walked fifteen blocks to the public library with the sweater tucked into my backpack. I didn't cry until I got to the basement, where I used to hide for hours with stacks of books. When I wandered through the stacks again, Jeff Houser and Paul Kenny followed me. They watched me from the other side of the shelves, then pushed books on top of my head. They were at the library because kids played kissing games after school in the adjoining graveyard.

"Where's your yellow sweater, faggot?"

I sat down in the young adult section, where the books would be lighter. I covered my head with both hands as their bombs fell all around me. Finally, they lost interest. I reshelved the books and walked home.

Once inside my bedroom, I closed the door and put on the sweater. I pulled my head inside the neckhole and pulled the sleeves all the way over my fists.

Before we went out to dinner that night, Dad announced that Mom was running late. Every time we left the house as a family unit, Dad called Mom a "cliffhanger." Truth was, Dad always held things up.

As I got into the backseat, Dad turned around and said, "That sweater's faggy."

"It's his color, Bev," Mom said. "It's *your* color, too. You're both autumns." Then she gunned the car out of the driveway.

It seemed ludicrous to me that Dad would weigh in on my outfit, since he was colorblind. Mom had to carefully monitor him in the morning so he didn't twist out of the house in some outfit that would make everyone at his office think Mom was sleeping late. It was not uncommon for Dad to think that combining plaid pants, a striped shirt, and a paisley tie was a good idea.

Dad and I sat across from each other at the restaurant. I was picking every fight I could. The fastest way to an entertaining argument with Dad was to make bratty comments about unilateral demilitarization or atheism. Dad sipped two glasses of cognac and made womanizing comments to the waitress. I'd never seen him like this.

The Colonel had broken dozens of bones jumping out of planes. He drank all of his life to ease chronic back pain, which was so excruciating that some mornings he had trouble getting out of bed. The first time I realized that Dad was older than most fathers was when I was four. We were wrestling and his back popped. The Colonel lay flat on the floor. I climbed atop his chest and couldn't understand why it was time to stop playing.

During his third brandy, Dad pointed at me and said he could kick my little ass. He gulped the rest of that lighter fluid and announced that it was time for us to leave.

Later I heard Mom and Dad talking in bed. I couldn't make out what they were saying—even with a glass against the door—but it went on for several hours.

That night, my mother started preparing the way for me. From that point on, she corrected Dad when he used antigay epithets. She called him into the bedroom when there were gay people on *Oprah* or *Donahue*. Mom must have really scared him, because the next morning—I swear to God—Dad wore yellow pants to the office.

hiding places

After much political maneuvering around my parents, I moved upstairs into my brother's old room, which was possibly the most amazing room a twelve-year-old could ever have. My parents were downstairs, so I had the run of the second floor. After much additional debate, I got a phone. I even had a stereo system, which I'd assembled piece by piece with yard-mowing money. There was a balcony where I could sneak cigarettes and gaze at the stars. Most importantly, there was a tiny studio connected to my room where I wrote on a computer that Hunter had given me.

I didn't get a padlock for my trunk until I was fourteen, so I had to be creative when it came to stashing my most sacred possessions. Luckily, the room featured several closets and crawl spaces. Hunter is thirteen years older than I am, so he was out of college and married by the time I found his amazing hiding places.

There were wall slats he'd loosened for storage, as well as removable floorboards and wooden boxes with tiny suitcase locks. I had a treasure trove of secret relics, accumulated over the years since I was five years old. The stash would have been enough to give both my parents cardiac arrest. Hidden in my room were

- Two cigars, stolen from the pockets of visiting generals.
- King Edward Cigars I bought at Lucerne's grocery store before
    Virginia initiated a smoking age.
- A pack of Barclay cigarettes which I took from my mother's
    purse.
- Watermelon gum to disguise my breath.
- Three little bottles of Jack Daniels I'd stolen from an airline
    attendant's cart on my way to Florida.
- A deck of nude male playing cards my mother received as a
    gag gift.
- A jock strap I stole from my father.
- A box of assorted underwear I'd lifted, one at a time, from the
    suitcases of our frequent houseguests.
- Trojan Enz condoms, which smelled vile. I poached these one
    at a time from my father's underwear drawer.
- A manila envelope full of Jim Palmer underwear ads I'd
    clipped out of magazines.
- A "marital aid" vibrator I found in my parents' room.
- Harold Robbins's *The Storyteller*, the spine of which was
    cracked in all the correct places.
- A beat-up copy of *Penthouse Letters* that Mason Emore gave
    me on my eleventh birthday.
- The Rudy Ray Moore *Zodiac* album, featuring the Sensuous
    Black Woman screaming, "That's right, gimme *all* that good
    dick."
- A bra and panties I'd taken from my sister's room.

Of all the things my mother could have found, the bra and
panties were the toughest to explain. I stuffed them in the woofer
of a stereo speaker and replaced the front panel.

One afternoon she entered my room with the undergarments
in hand.

"I found these in your speaker," she said.

I panicked. There was no explanation.

I had been curious about how they would look and feel. For reasons unbeknownst to me, I hid them, even though my sister's room was right across the hall. My sister didn't even live at home anymore. There was no good reason to horde.

"You're experimenting," Mom said.

I wanted to crawl inside the speaker myself and crank the Circle Jerks as loud as it would go. I said nothing. Mom left quietly. I wondered what else she'd found. I wondered whether I should get rid of everything. I wondered if she'd tell Dad.

The following week, when I was snooping in my sister's drawers again, I saw the same bra and panties. We couldn't discuss it at the time because neither of us had the words. I was startled to see those items in the drawer where Mom knew I'd return. It felt, mostly, like a blessing.

He touched boys.

I'd heard that Joel put his hands up the shirts and down the pants of several of my sixth-grade classmates. I was never much of a video game person, but when I heard these rumors, I visited that game room on an almost daily basis. I stared at the manager, Joel, every time he walked by, jingling a white apron full of quarters.

Being anointed in this dingy little chapel of diversion involved Joel clinking down three quarters on the tilted glass before you. An offering. An invitation, perhaps. It meant Joel noticed you.

After two weeks, I was growing impatient. I'd logged my initials as the seventh highest scorer on Ms. Pac Man, my game of choice. I was getting proficient in Frogger as well, but other boys were hearing a lot more quarters clink than I was. These boys, some of whom were the very ones rumored to have been felt up, were connoisseurs of Pole Position, Galaga, and other games involving driving or guns. Boy games, to be blunt. Ms. Pac Man and Frogger were girl games, geek games at best.

I followed Joel into the bathroom. I shot him looks. I tried to initiate conversation, which was no small task. There were, I learned, solid intellectual reasons why this man was operating a video arcade for pre-adolescents. I think he knew I was slumming.

It was the first of many times I would be willing to jettison my intelligence in pursuit of carnal delights.

Thing is, I was having no luck. I couldn't even get molested in this town. I refused, on principle, to obliterate space stations and rev engines in the hopes that my efforts would lead to a back-room diddle from a greasy, dirty-nailed manager with arrested development. I was twelve, but I knew tacky.

black balloon

In seventh grade, Neil and I went to Lexington High School for their talent show because Neil's brother was doing something or other. I don't recall what. I just remember hearing the MC announce the name Jesse Fowler. The audience shifted in their seats and whispered louder than they had between any other acts.

Jesse was then in tenth grade, so I only saw him occasionally around town. He had become infamous for dressing up as Boy George. Jesse was our town's queer Boo Radley. Even I had invoked horrible words against him.

Like Jesse, the middle-school librarian was fanatical about Boy George, so fanatical that she used to go to conventions where people would dress like him. She even came to school with her hair in Boy George's signature braids and brightly colored bows. She caked on makeup and lip-synched Culture Club songs at school assemblies. In her, Jesse had found the perfect Salieri for his Mozart.

The curtain opened on Jesse, who was dressed in a white tee shirt and baggy black pants. His hair was slicked back. He looked more standard issue than I'd ever seen him look. He was holding a black helium balloon. As a chorus of voices sang the song's refrain, "Too bad," I identified the voice of the lead singer. It was Boy George from Culture Club.

"Tooooooo . . . bad . . . ."

Jesse released the black balloon. It rose quickly toward the ceiling, until even its black ribbon slipped out of view. There was a collective gasp. Even this rough-and-tumble Rockbridge County audience could appreciate a moment of stage poetry. Jesse shot a knowing smile to a friend in the audience.

Again, I watched him dance. Oh, could that boy dance. He'd learned to dance in front of his family, who knew that when *Fame* came on TV, it was time to push back the coffee table. But this time, the audience was less on his side. It was easier for them to applaud Michael Jackson than Boy George. Jesse was dancing to music by his own kind, and that was more threatening to these folks. Jesse won third.

Years later, Jesse told me the story behind that black balloon. On his way to the talent show, he'd found it tied to his mailbox.

"How evil!" Jesse had said. "Child, let me undo that."

Jesse was on his way home from school during the first semester of his freshman year. He only had four blocks to go. He could have gone through the bushes in back of school and saved ten minutes, but this route gave him a chance to smoke. Jesse loved to smoke.

A green Jeep pulled up beside him. Craig Staton, the guitarist for the local heavy metal band Malachai, was driving. Simon Gardano, the band's lead singer, jumped out and kicked Jesse to the ground. Jesse curled into a ball until Simon was finished kicking him. Word flew around school the next day that Simon had kicked the little faggot's ass. Teachers heard about it. Nothing happened to Simon.

That summer, I got into a fight with Simon's little brother Jason. He'd called me a faggot at the pool. We tussled. His father was a coach at a local college, so both boys were feisty and enormous.

I'd been taking karate at VMI and was a green belt. I was eight years younger than all the cadets, so I was accustomed to fighting guys twice my size. Jason and I wrestled. He issued a "come on, faggot" and I kicked him in the stomach hard enough to make him double over. Then, to the amazement of the small crowd that had gathered, I spun around and did a fancy combination kick. I got him right in the face. His head smashed against the side mirror of a parked car. I hadn't practiced my fancy kick quite enough, so I toppled over and rolled ten feet down the hill. The kids laughed at me.

Then they saw the blood on Jason's hands. When I saw it, I rushed up and apologized. We'd both had enough. We walked to the lifeguard together and Jason went to the hospital.

When I think about those two brothers, I can't help but believe in karma, as woo-woo as that sounds. Gay bruises were paid for with a brother's blood. It makes me feel better to think of it as cosmic revenge, I have to admit. But only a little.

meet the press

Jesse once told me that there were many places he just didn't set foot during his four years at LHS.
"There were too many evil people," he said. "I got screamed at every time I walked into a room. I felt like I was wearing a strobe light on my head." I knew exactly what he meant, but my strobe started blinking years before high school. And it wasn't because I was gay.

My oldest brother was the commonwealth's attorney and had, in the spirit of the Reagan regime, led a full-tilt boogie grand jury investigation to root out drugs, pornography, and the people who loved them. This meant dragging dozens of teenagers, including our own sister, into court for invasive questioning.

My brother was already well-known for being an aggressive potty mouth in the courtroom. Needless to say, my family was unpopular with many of the people whose friends and loved ones had been busted, harassed, or simply mortified on the witness stand. I felt sure those people hated my guts. I saw the way people looked at us when we left the house. My mother wore dark glasses to the grocery store on days when something really mean had run in that morning's *Roanoke Times*.

Kids at school teased me relentlessly after my brother's name was printed above the words "The Only Dope in Town" on a widely circulated bumper sticker. So there were places I didn't go, places I knew people's laser-like stares would burn holes in my skin. If they got me alone, I figured they would cover my mouth with duct tape and throw me in the trunk of their car. I'd seen that in a movie once.

Even now, when I go home to Lexington, I wonder who in the restaurant has relatives in prison for drug charges brought against them during those days. I wonder how many times they'd punch me and I wonder what they'd say while they did it.

My parents kept me fairly sheltered from what was happening, but we got lots of crank calls, hang-ups, and threats. Finally, Mom called the police and we had our phone tapped. I thought this was extremely cool and invited friends over to listen to the clicks our phone made. My friends were impressed.

I saw my family on the evening news night after night. I saw the Colonel break into tears and repeat to the cameras, over and over, "I love my son. I love my son." Mom didn't comment, nor did my brother's wife.

Secretly, I wanted to be interviewed. I spent hours fashioning snappy, heartbreaking sound bites that, in my mind, would prompt officials to drop proceedings altogether. Somehow, I was determined to emerge from the turmoil as the real star.

I set up a podium in my room by turning a bookshelf on its side, then used a rubber-banded bundle of Magik Markers as microphones. This is how press conferences looked on TV, so I wanted to be ready. I worked up tears as I told the press they were destroying my family and paused from time to time so that the imaginary reporters could write down every word.

Roanoke Times reporter Anne Pettit wrote countless investigative pieces on the whole drama. Now that I've worked as a journalist myself, I can see she was only doing her job. But at the time, I wanted her dead. Once a week she'd call the house for comment, which upset my parents. She wrote front-page stories talking about things I wasn't even supposed to know about humanity yet. My parents had me rehearse saying "no comment." It was a phrase I knew I'd never use.

Then things got ugly. A story broke alleging that my brother had molested lots of women. I didn't know much about it, because my parents started hiding the front page of the newspaper on certain days. I'd come down for breakfast and my father would give me a pep talk about what to say when kids mentioned the brouhaha. "Say you love your brother. Just say you love your brother."

That's when I started cutting up Anne Pettit. I had the same dream over and over for years. I still have it sometimes.

I run into her down by Wood's Creek. She's been following me home from school. She asks me a rapid procession of questions and I say "no comment." Every day, it's the same. She follows me home from school and I say "no comment."

I kick her feet out from under her, strangle her, and dig my knees into her chest to keep her from moving. I pull her hair hard enough so that some comes loose in my hand, making her eyes widen—all the while saying "I love my brother. I love my brother."

Eventually, my brother was disbarred. Several times, actually, but it got so Shakespearean that I'll save the rest for the campfire. Suffice it to say that the experience dragged on throughout my teens. My brother stopped making the front page, but people never stopped staring at me, if for different reasons.

But I already knew how to deal with that. I learned to enjoy the attention. I imagined that everyone who stared at me had a camera. I couldn't possibly accommodate all of their questions. I was a celebrity, after all. They were staring at *me*. People who stare are more often curious than hateful. And if they're staring, you must be doing something right.

keys

While friends of mine were toking up in middle school, I had to borrow oblivion from my parents' vast liquor cabinet one half-inch at a time. Mom and Dad never noticed.

I supplied my friends with booze when we snuck out. We'd meet at our old elementary school at 2 A. M. and I'd share my thermos of "speedball," a blend of every conceivable type of liquor. For some reason, it never occurred to us to use mixers. All of my parents' friends drank their liquor straight. My father's very dry martinis were nothing but vodka. I rarely drank the stuff, because it was dag nasty. I was content to feed and watch. After downing the concoction, my friends would throw up, grow violent, and attract police attention for breaking curfew. I think we all would have been better off sharing a joint.

I was curious, but in my mind, trying pot would have been a betrayal of my family. The Colonel had scared me into believing that reporters would give me drugs so they could get me arrested and embarrass the family.

I got my first whiff of pot at a Grateful Dead concert that my sister took me to in Maryland. As the band launched into "Ripple," the hippies in front of us screamed, "They haven't played this in *years!*" Then they fired up a bowl. I looked around for reporters.

The first time I smoked pot was at another Dead show I went to with my brother.

One of my serious finds in my brother's closet had been a metal pipe he'd made out of plumbing hardware. His resourcefulness never ceased to amaze me. The pipe held a deep fascination for me. I would later learn that my father had found the pipe and punched my brother in the face with it. The one thing you never said to the Colonel was the F-word. My father threw the pipe into the yard, and the next day my brother retrieved it.

Rooting around my sister's room, I had found a ceramic dish of potpourri, which turned out to be slightly antique sweet leaf. I had carefully bagged it and carved a hiding place between the floor boards, which I covered with additional carpet. I had learned early on that when you have siblings, it pays to snoop.

My brother had left me alone in the parking lot at the Dead show so that he could go off and scalp some extra tickets. I think he traded those tickets for a big bag of pot, but I wasn't supposed to know. He certainly wasn't going to corrupt his fourteen-year-old brother. Not directly, anyway.

I packed the pipe, sitting in the front seat of my mother's station wagon, which I called the Brady Wagon. I took a deep hit, as I'd heard one was supposed to. I didn't cough it up and chased the hit with a big slurp of grape soda. I took several more tokes, then carefully wrapped up the pipe and hid it in the bottom of my backpack. I figured I'd walk around the parking lot and buy some tie-dye shirts. Nobody gets stoned their first time, anyway.

I got stoned the first time, to say the least. I wandered off into the circus, smiling at strangers and wishing that someone would talk to me. I ate a large bowl of peanut butter-and-broccoli soup, which forever cured me of my aversion to broccoli. When I returned to the car, my brother was sitting on the bumper, hand outstretched.

"Gimme the keys, bruh."

I reached in my pockets but couldn't find the keys. He covered his eyes with one hand and bit his fingernails. I frantically searched every pocket, but by this point, I knew what had happened.

I looked through the passenger window and saw the keys dangling from the ignition. My buzz was killed. My brother had a terrible temper when it came to cars. I wanted to go for a walk and come back when he was finished. I suggested this, princess that I was. He growled at me, then managed to break in with a coat hanger and twigs—twigs! I found this messianic. He put the keys in my hand and closed my fingers around them.

"I want you to do something for me," he said. "Whenever you're getting out of a car, shake the keys in your hand. Make sure you hear them jingle."

I still jingle my keys, although the last time I spoke with AAA, they said I'd used up my roadside service allotment for the year. So I'm far from cured.

Pat Robertson and I both grew up in Lexington, Virginia. I think God put me on this planet to balance him out. I've got my work cut out for me.

He played football at Lexington High School with Dad, who was an even more unlikely footballer than I was. Dad was scrawny and wore glasses, but I imagine that he was scrappy.

Once, a man approached him in the bank lobby and asked if Dad remembered who he was.

Dad replied, "I broke your leg in the Buena Vista game fifty years ago." This from the man who flinched every time I sassed a referee.

In 1988, Pat threw his pointy white hat into the presidential race and invited my parents to a luncheon at the Homestead resort. The Colonel came home starry-eyed, drunk on Pat's notoriety. Dad was easily impressed by remarkably unimpressive people. My mother, on the other hand, set her purse down on the radiator with a thud.

"How was lunch?" I asked.

"What an asshole," Mom said. My eyes lit up because it was the first time I'd ever heard her use that word. I sat down on the steps to watch.

"Don't be vulgar," Dad said. "He's a Christian."

"A Christian doesn't go on and on about his horses and wealth and jewelry," she barked. "Pat Robertson is not *my kind* of Christian."

My father saw that she was poisoning my young mind and attempted to placate her. There was no placating my mother.

"I'd rather vote for one of his goddamn horses," she said.

"Don't talk like that in front of the boy," Dad said, banging his fist on the radiator cover.

My mother went into the living room and slammed the door. This signaled the end of a fight and the Colonel knew it. We had solid wooden doors and their impact always got the dogs barking.

A slamming door was Dad's cue to go to his sister's house. She would remind him that he was a handsome citizen-soldier. Such reassurances were frequent from my aunt. She was a major reason that my parents had such a successful marriage. Thanks to her, my father knew better than to try to win fights with my mother.

After Dad left, I went into the kitchen where Mom was loading the dishwasher. "Was he that slimy?" I asked.

"I feel like I need to take a shower," she said.

Once upon a time, in a not-so-far-away land, Mom was a rabid Republican. She spent twenty years organizing fundraisers, handing out lawn posters, and stumping for pasty white Southern men. These people regularly filled our backyard for cocktail chatter about whatever cultural genocide they were plotting that election season.

My parents would vote for Reagan both times. For the Colonel, who'd been in three wars, the Cold War's Red Scare was persuasive. Though Dad considered himself a Southern Democrat, he happily voted for the character actor who promised to spend billions bringing video games to young military recruits.

Children inherit the politics of their parents until they are able to leave family loyalty outside the voting booth. By the time I was of voting age, my mother had become disgusted with the fever-pitch hatred of the Republican party.

After seeing Pat Buchanan's 1992 Republican convention speech and Barbara Bush's amused reaction, Mom was furious. She loved the First Lady because they both had English Springer

Spaniels, but there was Barbara, laughing at Buchanan's homophobic speech—the last straw for my mother.

Mom started going to local Democratic meetings, where the other folks initially believed her to be a spy. Republican party phone banks still call her on a weekly basis, asking for cash. Her voice goes baritone as she tells the hapless minimum-wage operator more than s/he ever cared to know about gay rights.

These days, Mom and I vote together. She still calls Pat Robertson the "nouveau riche asshole."

When I was twelve, I'd bugged my parents to let me have a paper route and they'd refused. Hunter had had a paper route, which was remembered in our household as a Mistake. Whenever he got sick, one of my parents had to drive him on his route as he rubber-banded, folded, and tossed.

My parents were fifteen years older now—Mom in her forties and Dad in his sixties. They were over paper routes and wanted me to find another rite of passage.

For two weeks during the summer after sixth grade, I naïvely agreed to take a friend's route, which was seventy houses for fifty dollars a week. Getting up at dawn was bad enough, but carrying around seventy newspapers in a canvas bag was decidedly unglamorous work. After the very first day, I went home and slept for three hours. I don't know how kids do this before school. When I woke up, I told my mother I was glad she'd vetoed my taking a permanent route.

"I know it's hard being raised by a perfect mother," she said. It was one of her favorite lines.

With each step, I felt the weight of the blaze orange strap digging into alternating shoulders. I started throwing the papers hard at front doors. If I was up, I figured everyone ought to be. There was something satisfying about hitting a door hard enough to rouse noisy pets.

Three days into my route, my mind became a calculator. Seventy houses at fifty dollars a week was around seventy cents a house. Seven times a week meant that each time I threw a paper, I was making a dime. Two hours each morning meant that I was making a little more than three dollars and fifty cents an hour. That didn't include the time it took to collect money from the rich white women who made me come back three times before they had a check in hand. I had my calculations down to fractions of pennies per footstep. How do newspapers get away with this sort of child slavery?

The house in which Pat Robertson grew up is across the street from the old high school, which is now an elementary school. It's next to Grandma Entsminger's house, where Dad took me on holidays. My biological grandparents and her own grandchildren were all dead, so Grandma Entsminger and I adopted one another. I gently tucked her paper behind the screen door.

The first time I delivered a paper to Pat's childhood home, I stood on the patio and held the paper a foot above my head. I spat, then wound up like a pitcher. It was a Wednesday paper, a good one in terms of heft and velocity. I anchored my right foot on a geranium pot and let it fly. I watched with glee as it careened end over end toward the door.

But it didn't hit the door. Instead of a wake-up thud, I heard glass shatter. I'd taken out one of the small windows alongside the door. Glass spilled everywhere.

At the time, it didn't occur to me that I was breaking Pat Robertson's window. I didn't know he was attributing floods and hurricanes to little old me. I didn't know he was encouraging parents to send their kids to "ex-gay" centers where they would be tortured and brainwashed. I didn't know how many gay kids would take their lives because people like Pat Robertson said they were on the highway to hell.

That window cost me my entire two-week's salary. In hindsight, it was worth every dime.

I'd already stolen a pair of his underwear. This was

part of my routine when we had a male houseguest. This one
was different, though. Mr. Miller was blind.

He and Dad knew each other somehow, probably from VMI
or the military. That's how the Colonel knew everybody.

Mom had been joking for the past week that she was going to
serve dinner in her bra and panties.

"He won't be able to tell," she said.

"Goddamn it, woman." Dad called Mom "woman" when he
was joking, on steroids after a surgery, or deadly serious.

True to her threat, Mom came out in a white silk slip for after-
dinner drinks. Dad waved his hands at her and tightened his
face like he was violently constipated, but Mom just kept talking to Mr. Miller, jiggling her boobs like a go-go dancer.

That night, as Mr. Miller prepared for his shower, I slipped
inside the bathroom and sat on the wicker hamper to wait for him.
I was thirteen but determined.

I watched him undress from my seat by the window. He stepped
into the shower and soaped up. Never is a man more humble than
when he thinks he's alone. He scrubbed the stretch marks around
his belly and fumbled with the shampoo bottle.

As he lathered up his hair, I unzipped my pants and started
to jerk off. I wanted to burn the image of this naked man into

my brain for future use. But seeing him in the shower wasn't arousing. My voyeurism made me feel guilty, but since I'm not Catholic, guilt is not a turn-on. *I shouldn't be watching this.* I felt more alone than ever. It was pathetic, really. The only way I could find sex was to steal it from the blind.

I tiptoed to the door, then opened it as quietly as I could. Mr. Miller looked up from his suds.

Trying to feign a mistaken entrance, I said, "Oh, I'm sorry," and closed the door behind me.

I knew I'd stolen something more valuable than underwear from this man—his privacy. I removed the pair of size 42 Hanes from their hiding place beneath the floorboards in my room and crept across the hall. Once in his room, I tucked the briefs back into his suitcase, exactly where I'd found them.

Rich was my best friend during my eighth-grade year.

We met at a Guadalcanal Diary concert at the Washington & Lee University pavilion. I was thirteen and snuck under the rail into the beer garden. I was doing my best Drew Barrymore impersonation, coaxing sips of everyone's beers. Rich was the first person to hand me his cup and let me finish it. He fetched more beer for me but counted so I wouldn't go home trashed. He was always counting.

I started hanging out with him almost every day. We went on drives through the mountains and played squash. We talked about philosophy and music. He challenged me in ways that kids my age just didn't. Their primary concerns seemed to be kissing and sports.

Since I'd already gone through the whole spin-the-bottle phase in sixth grade with older kids, I was bored. Besides, my peers were doing polite peck-on-the-lips stuff. When I learned to play, we were doing tongues and feeling boobs.

The first time a girl French-kissed me, I pulled away and said, "That's disgusting!" Kissing girls never really grew on me, apart from the taboo thrill of sharing intimacies late at night, after curfew, with the constant threat of a sweeping police floodlight. For some gay men, the allure of that rush is intoxicating throughout their lives. While I totally understand that, I was pretty much over it by eighth grade.

---

how i learned to snap **41**

Rich treated me like a peer. He listened to me in ways that no adult ever had. I could talk to him about punk, cry about my family, and bitch about how meaningless school was.

The first time he called me his little brother was the day I started writing. I filled notebooks with precious, all-caps accounts of every conversation, hug, and fight that we ever shared. I logged the number of Diet Cokes and beers we had between us. I wrote down what albums played on our drive to the 9:30 Club in D.C. to see Marshall Crenshaw, the Slickee Boys, and Pianosauras, a band that played toy instruments. When the band smashed up their miniature guitars at the end of their set, Rich retrieved a fretboard for me.

Because of the beer, I knew I couldn't tell my friends about him. I didn't want him to get in trouble. A friend of my parents lived near Rich and had already told my father she smelled beer on my breath. The next night I threw rocks at that bitch's window almost hard enough to break the glass. But my parents still didn't know what was going on. Mom was my go-to girl, the parent to ask for permission on most matters. She had an inkling.

Nights I saw Rich, we'd listen to obscure records, drink beer, and talk. We talked about literature. He gave me a copy of *A Catcher in the Rye*. We talked about my future. But mostly, we talked about my family. Rich rarely spoke of his own background. To this day, he remains somewhat of a riddle.

I was limited to three beers on a school night, which was all for the best. My family's colorful shenanigans were definitely enough to inspire excess. Beer was great therapy, and it never got out of hand.

Rich taught me to drive right after I turned fourteen. His car was an automatic and it was much easier than the time I'd tried driving a stick shift with Shelley and Regina, all drunk.

About a year into our friendship, Rich and I were inseparable. He picked me up from school sometimes and took me driving through the Blue Ridge Mountains. What with all my family's drama, he calmed me down on several near-suicidal occasions.

He was the big brother I'd always wanted. My three brothers were so much older and left home long before I could have much of a relationship with any of them. One lived on TV and in my mind. One had a family. And the third was born-again, so what was I gonna do? It's hard to have a relationship with someone who thinks you're going to hell and says as much. My born-again brother called my bedroom the "den of Satan" because its walls were covered with posters of my favorite rock icons. When he came to visit, he affixed enormous teddy bear stickers over their faces, so as not to traumatize his young Christian children. The first major fight we had was when his teddy bear sticker ripped my picture of Rob Halford from Judas Priest. I kissed Rob every night before I went to bed. He was my first leather daddy, and my brother had literally defaced him.

I hugged Rich almost every night before I walked home from his apartment. If I'd been crying, the hugs lasted a long time as he blew cool air on my neck. Then, whether I was upset or not, they just lasted longer.

This was one of our longest hugs. R.E.M.'s *Chronic Town* EP was playing on Rich's stereo, which automatically flipped over cassettes at the end of each side. We'd already heard the twenty-minute album three times that night, but we just let it keep going.

"Suspicion yourself, suspicion yourself, don't get caught," repeated the singer.

The window shades were all the way down, as they always were. We were both shaking, and our hands slowly slipped down each other's backs.

"Gentlemen, don't get caught."

We didn't kiss. We could feel the hard-ons through our pants. We'd felt these same protrusions for months. A few weeks before, I had hugged him goodnight while wearing a pair of shorts and popped a mortifying tent in his front yard. Finally, our hands came to rest on each other. We unzipped and finally, tentatively, we touched.

"I could live a million."

We stroked each other slowly, then frantically, like dogs. We'd been living with this unnamed tension for a year now. We couldn't hold off any longer.

"We stumble through the A . . . B . . . C . . . "

My cum hit two metal folding chairs by the window. It sounded like a bird falling to its death on a tin roof, then bouncing. Comets dancing with broken feet. We laughed as we wiped it up later, my first evidence that there was a life outside the city limits of Lexington, Virginia.

That album goes everywhere with me. Every time I see it, I buy it. I have it on vinyl, CD, and cassette. I never tire of the murky lyrics, most of which I can't make out. Obscure, muddy, buried— the perfect soundtrack of a burgeoning adolescence.

That embrace was the most mutual, consensual sexual act I've had in my entire life. Everything since has felt less pure.

The first time I walked into Flip Side Records, I was thirteen years old. The owners were playing Joe

Jackson's *Night and Day* on one of the brand-new CD players. I'd
never seen a compact disc before.

"I stepped into another world," Jackson sang.

The album was one of two hundred records my sister had given
me when she was researching her senior thesis at Hollins College
several years before. Tipper Gore had turned the topic of rock's
deleterious effects on youth into fast food for pundits, so my sister sat her then ten-year-old brother down with a stack of ques-
tionnaires. I ranked each song for lyrical content, looking for
sex, drugs, and violence. In the process, I got to hear Blue Öys-
ter Cult, the Pretenders, Lords of the New Church, and a slew
of other bands. It was arguably the most important education I've
ever received.

Joe Jackson was one of my favorites. I'd listened to *Night and
Day* over and over, staring at the cover art and dreaming of the
day I could move to Manhattan. I traced the line drawing of Joe
Jackson sitting at his piano into my notebook. In my version, I was
sitting next to him.

"This album came out when I was in third grade," I announced,
shuffling past the three clerks behind the counter.

"I heard *that!*" Rhonda said, taking a long drag off her Marlboro Red.

"Third grade?" the two men said in unison.

I proceeded to reel off the song titles in order, the producer, the record company, and the year of release. I was 100%, grade-A obnoxious.

I stayed for two hours, lecturing them about everything from Afghanistan to Led Zeppelin. At five, Rhonda went home. Wade and Price let me stay long after closing, sensing that a thirteen-year-old with that much talking to do needed whatever encouragement they could muster.

I kept showing up at Flip Side like a bad penny. I went in every day after school, talking to Rhonda until Wade and Price arrived at five to close up. Rhonda was a down-home girl. She lived hard and had an enormous boyfriend who had a shaved head, tattoos, and a penchant for trouble. Every day, Rhonda served up dizzying stories of the previous night—how she'd gotten thrown out of a vehicle as it flipped over, how she'd tossed full beer cans at rival NASCAR fans, how she'd gotten in a fight at the drive-in with a girl who had hair so long that Rhonda wrapped her fist in it and "got down to business."

Wade and Price were mild-mannered by comparison. They'd both recently graduated from college. The record store was a sort of hobby to supplement their new careers. The store had been a head shop in the seventies, selling everything from black velvet Santana tapestries to "pussy-scented" incense.

Wade and Price were trying to change the store into a place where college students would buy music. There was a small but growing bin of independent label and punk records. I scooped up albums by Agnostic Front, the Coolies, and Robyn Hitchcock. I quickly became Flip Side's most loyal customer. If not in dollars, definitely in hours.

Wade and Price were twice my age, so they took responsibility for filling in the gaps in my education. They handed me books by Thoreau and Byron. They taught me who Edmund Burke was and quizzed me on which Beatles album contained any given song. Pretty soon, I was in the store so often that people assumed I worked there. When I turned fourteen, I filled out the child labor paperwork for part-time employment and took a job there.

My first Saturday behind the counter, I nearly lost a major customer. At the risk of dating myself, we did not yet have those little credit card swipey machines. There was a very complicated procedure for looking up credit card numbers, calling in for authorization, and writing down the last five digits—I couldn't remember to save my life how to go about any of it.

The customer, a snooty Washington & Lee professor, glared at me as I fumbled with his credit card and suggested that "children should be lifeguards, not in customer service."

I said something equally rude—but not nearly as clever—and the man vowed to return to the store only on days when the help was "of age."

At night, after Wade and Price closed up, we'd drink beer and gossip about all the high society townspeople. I had to sit on the floor behind the counter because police officers frequently walked by and shone flashlights in the store windows to make sure we weren't burglars.

As I became more of a fixture on the staff, I grew more meddlesome. When Wade and Price arrived for the closing shift, I'd present them with a detailed catalog of backlist albums no store should be without: the Rolling Stones's *Let It Bleed*, AC/DC's *Back in Black*, Carole King's *Tapestry*. In my excitement, I'd list hundreds upon hundreds of absolutely essential albums, then scream at them for not stocking the store properly. I had no idea Flip Side was about to go out of business.

My lists encompassed their personal lives as well. Wade had struggled to lose weight, so I routinely mapped out week-long diets and woke him up every morning at 6 A.M. to go jogging.

Wade's plump stature and receding hairline caused him a lot of grief. Price routinely called him "fat boy" or "baldie." Wade would return the favor by calling Price "short shit" or "four eyes." Do men ever grow out of that?

My five siblings were all at least a dozen years older than I was. By the time I needed siblings most, they were starting their own families so I adopted Wade and Price as older brothers and expected them to perform sibling duties on a daily basis. These duties included providing beer, watching my soccer games, and enduring emergency phone conversations that stretched into hours.

My parents were initially suspicious of two adult men who were interested in spending so much time with a fourteen-year-old. Mom could tell beer was involved, and the Colonel occasionally called me at the store to demand that I get home *right this minute*. Rationed beer was the first compromise Mom and I ever made. I somehow sold her on a quasi-European view of drinking, telling her about all the intellectual conversations that one or two beers facilitated. She relented, silently allowing me to hang out at the store as long as I was stealthy about Dad.

Mom asked the inevitable question—why would Wade and Price want to spend time with a teenager? I told her they were like brothers, that they listened to me, and that I needed them. I was sitting on the edge of her bed, gathering the comforter in my clenched hands. Mom looked back at the TV screen, took a long breath, and said, "O.K., honey." Mom knew I needed to fly.

Years later, she told me that she saw me creep down the steps night after night to sneak out with my friends. She let me go because she imagined that I had some idea of what I was doing. It worried her, naturally. She'd look up from the covers and see a shadow of her son creeping into the streets at 2 A. M.. But she let me go.

My friends regarded my relationships with Wade and Price as mysterious and strange. Some of the boys called them the Flip Side Faggots. A few of my girlfriends had similar relationships with college students and adults. We bonded over the familial ties we'd managed to create. Every morning in Latin, Missy and I passed each other notes about the contact we'd had with our adopted older brothers. Our teacher was close enough to senility that we could get away with one note each. But even she was quick to spot crime, so one note was all.

Missy and I talked about what their apartments looked like, what they got us for our birthdays, what nicknames they'd concocted for us. We knew we wouldn't think the other weird for subscribing so adamantly to foster fraternity. We could gush and brag and paean, all in the syrupy language of eighth-grade cursive.

The Saturday Wade and Price told me the store was closing, I'd put an especially long stock order together. It was all very dramatic. My puppy dog tears rolled right down my face and turned the fountain ink of my order into a moody landscape.

Two months later, at Christmas, after my family had finished opening all of our gifts, Mom led me into the guest bedroom. There was a tall wrapped present leaning against the wall.

"This was delivered for you," she said.

I knew it was from the guys at Flip Side, since there hadn't been presents from them under the tree. I was more excited about this gift than any other, and I tore off the paper with a single pull.

Mom started crying before I did. It was the blue wooden sign that hung over the store's awning. In gold leaf, the words *Flip Side* surrounded a large record. It must have weighed fifty pounds.

"I don't know what you're going to do with that thing," she said.

I touched the gold. I'd never touched it before because it was always ten feet in the air.

"That place was important to me, Mom," I said.

"I know it was," she said.

total theater

Mom had been urging me all summer to do something productive. Between seventh and eighth grade, I'd mowed lawns and read *Less Than Zero*. It was the summer that MTV came to Lexington cable, so I replaced pro wrestling with David Lee Roth and Madonna. This was not a cultural golden age for me. I certainly wasn't reading Flaubert by candlelight.

Earlier that summer, I had attended the city's free tennis clinic. I showed up the first day with my sister Lisa's tennis racquet, a wooden Chris Evert model. The handle read, in bold green letters, *Miss Chris*. The next day I returned with a different racquet, which had a generic aluminum frame. Nevertheless, Shane Mueller and Dale Shorter had me in tears for three days running, and ultimately I just didn't go back.

Our community theater needed a techie. I'd seen all the plays there since I was a kid, but it never occurred to me to be interested in theater. The people my age who did all that singing and dancing stuff struck me as child prodigies who'd been taking piano lessons since they could uncurl their fingers. I was just a big smart-ass. What good is that?

For several weeks, I painted chairs and rolled sets around. I stared admiringly at the men with tool belts who measured and jigsawed their way into my fantasies. I did whatever I was told, which ranged from fetching Mountain Dew to dismantling platforms. I didn't even know what play we were doing at first, because the cast rehearsed elsewhere for the first few weeks.

On the back wall, one of the W&L drama majors had spray-painted *Total Theater*. I asked our stage manager what that meant and she said, "It means you'll be poor, gay, and despised for the rest of your life."

People were always singing songs I'd never heard—peppy show tunes, ballads, and Barry Manilow songs. At a certain point, I just accepted being the youngest person in the room. When so many cultural references fly out from myriad bygone eras, you simply adjust to the noise.

Avery was an actor who was helping with the set construction for this show. He and I worked together every day. He taught me how to mix paint. He was older, extremely sweet, and always singing. Sometimes he sang songs right to me to see how fast he could get me to blush. It didn't take long. I never sang along with these strange gypsies. I was perfectly content to live backstage, where fellow techies shared arch, nasty jokes about the singers.

The week before opening night, Jesse Fowler joined the technical crew. I'd never actually talked to him at length before, but the very first day, Jesse clocked me. Five of us were sitting in a circle, backstage. The other four were discussing their careers after college. They spoke of Chicago, New York, and Los Angeles. They spoke of touring the country.

Avery turned to me and said, "Kirk, what do you want to be when you grow up?"

"I don't know," I said.

"I know what you're gonna be," Jesse said, lighting the cigarette he was only supposed to smoke outside.

Before I could say anything, our town's grand British *ac*-tress, swooped into the room and announced that her throat was closing up. She complained about this every night. She didn't even need to be in the same room as smoke or hairspray in order to be upset. She only had to *know it was happening*. Jesse gathered up his enormous black purse and perched on the back steps outside the theater, finishing his cigarette in exile.

I stared at him, taking in his chronically black wardrobe and his bleached-out bangs. I wanted to start smoking.

That night Jesse and I got yelled at by Ray Sanford, the director whose claim to fame was making everyone cry at least once. We'd rolled a set piece off in the middle of a song. The actress was a bitch, so it was somewhat intentional. Ray started ranting and stomping his feet like a child who'd been deprived of banana pudding. Jesse stood backstage, just out of Ray's sight range, and gave him the finger. Impressed, I too stuck my middle finger in the air. That's when I learned the old theater maxim: If you can see them, they can see you.

"Do you want to go home RIGHT NOW, young man? Because I don't NEED that sort of disrespect and I WON'T tolerate it."

"Child, go hide!" Jesse hissed.

I ran to the back of the shop and crawled under a sawhorse. Ray continued to lecture the cast about snotty attitudes and mutiny for the next fifteen minutes. I sat under the sawhorse, staring up at the wall that read "Total Theater." It was the first time Ray made me cry.

The night the play closed, the theater also closed for good. Closing nights are nostalgic enough, but people were digging through boxes holding twenty-plus years of history. They were taking home props and costumes, sorting through stacks of cast photos that had once been displayed in the lobby. I found a picture of Jesse and tucked it between the pages of my journal. I would need that picture more than he would.

A woman in the cast left a cooler of beer in the light booth. She mentioned it to me, but told me to keep quiet about it. That was the bargain for a fourteen-year-old—do what you want, but don't implicate the adults.

By my third beer, the party had disintegrated into yet another cast sing-a-long, with the lead actor on piano. Why, I wondered, would these people be interested in singing these songs yet again?

The actors crowded around the piano, singing each other's songs. The musical we'd done had some catchy songs, but the technical crew had spent the previous two weeks making fun of every line. As far as we were concerned, we'd pushed our last set.

Some of us moved the party over to the stage manager's apartment. Her boyfriend was incredibly cute, and I'd had a crush on him for three days. I had a crush on a different man every two days, so this qualified as a long-term romance. A girl with a virginal soprano voice was sitting in the middle of the sofa, smoking a clove cigarette. She patted her lap for me to sit down and gave me a drag. It burned my throat so severely that I started hacking. Fearing that I looked stupid and immature, I tried to feign some sort of freak dog dance, but people simply crinkled their noses at me, puzzled.

Several beers later, I was reaching my limit on being around actors. Yet again, we heard someone tell the story about Mitzi Stockwell, whose nickname, for some reason, was Sweet Potato. Someone had put a sweet potato in her prop lunchbox, instead of the expected corn muffins, prompting a full throttle rage-out from her co-star. It was funny when the crew did it, but the problem with actors is that they're used to doing things four hundred times before they get it right.

I grabbed my beer and headed for the door. Avery followed me out. He'd had enough, too. He was one of those people with really pretty voices who smokes a lot. I never figured that one out.

We walked to his apartment a few blocks away. I told him how sad I was that all of this was ending. I detailed some of my family's antics. I used the word *weird* in just about every sentence.

He fixed us fuzzy navels, which I'd never had before. He sat down behind me and put his hands on my shoulders. People in theater hugged each other. My puberty meant that the women stroked my hair, while the men tousled it. I'd never been touched so often.

His hands felt good, but I was shaking. Avery tried to soothe me by kneading my neck. I stared straight ahead into the half-empty glass of peachy orange. If I fixed my eyes hard enough on that orange, I thought, I could disappear into it.

"Do you want to go into the other room?" Avery asked.

I bowed my head, knowing that I was about to disappoint him. "I need to go home," I said.

Avery took his hands from my shoulders and stood up quickly. The drive home only lasted a few blocks. He probably shouldn't have been driving, and I wasn't old enough yet. On the way home he gave me advice on singing. He said I should try.

When he dropped me off, we hugged and said our goodnights. I went inside and threw up from nerves and booze. To this day, the mere suggestion of peaches makes my stomach dance.

how i learned to snap

Jesse Fowler was the gay Rosa Parks of Lexington, Virginia. In a way, he one-upped her. He got the bus driver fired. Much of what I know about dignity came from him.

Jesse was a senior when I was a freshman. After we became friends, we walked home from school together. Upon parting, I'd run home to write down everything he said. I worked feverishly to make his vocabulary my own. From him I learned to properly use the words *tragic, fierce,* and *drama*. I learned to begin, whenever possible, all sentences with *Child* . . . .

He had a different hairstyle every two weeks and often chided me for my "boy hair." He sometimes crimped my bangs, prompting the Colonel to ask if I'd been hanging out with the Fowler boy again.

"Yes," I replied at supper. "And *child,* he's *fierce.*"

One day, as we neared the corner of McDaniel Street where he walked east and I walked west, a school bus came to a rolling stop beside us. The bus was full of elementary school children. Dozens of them stuck their heads out the windows and screamed "Faggot!"

Jesse held his middle finger in the air for a solid minute. It felt like a lifetime. "I don't have enough middle fingers for these children," he said.

Finally, the bus sped off. Kids were hanging their heads out the windows, giving him the finger and screaming.

I asked him where they learned that word. "The bus driver tells them to call me that," he said. "It happens every day. I'm just trying to get from point A to point B."

"Every day?" I asked, wondering if they would start slowing down for me.

"Come with me," he said, lighting a cigarette.

We walked to his house. I felt like I was going backstage. He'd painted his entire room black. Besides the phase in which he dressed as Boy George, Jesse had done a stint as Robert Smith of the Cure, but that day he was looking one hell of a lot like Siouxsie Sioux. Throughout each transformation, he was unequivocally Jesse.

Jewelry and clothing was scattered everywhere. He had bottles of Sun-In. When I picked one up to look at it, he grabbed it from me.

"You've got brown hair like mine. Save yourself the pleasure of turning a very vivid orange, because you *so* will."

Jesse took several silver rings from his fingers and put them on his dresser.

He sat me on the bed and said, "Pay attention." He put the stereo needle down on Bronski Beat's *Smalltown Boy* and watched my face change as I heard Jimmy Somerville's voice for the first time. *The love that you need will never be found at home,* Jimmy sang. My soul already knew the song.

"Run away, turn away, run away, turn away, run away."

Jesse danced in the mirror. He'd taught the entire school to dance. The only problem was that our high school's soundtrack was a bluegrass ditty, his was a twelve-inch remix. He had a brand of soul that had eluded me altogether. His dancing was a joyful explosion, the genesis of which is authentic pain. He danced so well with black girls because their dancing was also about escaping. It was about showing people they wouldn't let the world win.

One of his signature expressions was "I am not afraid." That day, after being called faggot by dozens of screaming children, Jesse positioned me in front of the mirror. He taught me to make wide circles with my arm. Three circles and a snap, he said. Snap on the word *not*. "I am *not* (snap) afraid."

I practiced over and over.

"Let the children hear you," he said.

When I went home, I stood in front of my mirror. I snapped and snapped and snapped. I snapped for my parents, who thought it was a beatnik thing. I snapped for my white friends, who thought it was funny. I snapped for my black friends, who gave me advice on how to snap even louder—how to really scare people when I snapped. Because that was the purpose.

Later, Jesse went to the school board office and filed a complaint that eventually got that bus driver fired.

"I hope the bitch gets her food stamps," he said. It was the sweetest vengeance a small town queer could imagine in the late-eighties.

When all was said and done, Jesse just wanted to walk home in peace. The bravest of angels often travel with dignity as their only weapon. Jesse also packed a knife throughout high school, just in case.

Later that year, when Jesse graduated, people cheered as he crossed the stage. He'd put up with their shit for four long years. His chemically damaged hair poked out from under his scarlet cap. His pointy black boots carried him across that stage, each step eliciting another audience member's howl.

It was the end of my ninth-grade year. I still had three more to go. How in the world was I going to get from point A to point B? I am *not* afraid, I said out loud.

As he received his diploma, I could hear the angels snapping.

Once I started getting regular sex from Rich and diva lessons from Jesse, things slowly fell into place. But Rich and I never talked about what we were doing, and Jesse never said the word *gay* that I can remember. Jesse taught me how to be fierce. The rest I had to figure out on my own.

I started by "questioning" and filled several journals with endless navel-gazing. Thankfully, I had a foot locker with a padlock, so I was able to commit my self-examinations to paper without fear of discovery. Every teenager should have a trunk that locks.

Intergenerational sex saved my life. When I started having sex as a teenager, the daunting questions that ricocheted inside my skull ceased to be rhetorical. If it hadn't been for sex at such a young age, my questioning phase could have stretched on for years, and that would have gotten *really* tedious.

Sex with an older man probably sped up my coming-out process by years. If it hadn't been for Rich, I might have turned into a mopey Goth kid. The horror, the horror. Had our relationship been discovered, Rich could have done time in jail. During the time we were having sex, it never dawned on me that he was literally risking his freedom over me.

American culture's only frame of reference for sex with minors is abuse. I don't deny that abuse occurs, but this should be addressed on a case-by-case basis. A blanket approach that criminalizes all sex between adults and minors undermines the fact that for many gay teenagers, sex with an adult can be a beautiful, life-changing experience. It was for me.

I sought out sex with older men time and time again as a teenager. I had fumbling sexual encounters with other kids as a preadolescent, but they always left me unsatisfied. None of us knew what we were doing, and our shame and fear overwhelmed any joy of discovery. Kids should have the opportunity to discover their sexuality, whatever it may be, during puberty. That's not to say it won't shift around as they have a variety of sexual experiences throughout their lives. Puberty is the ideal time for parents and teachers to let kids know they're not going through these developmental stages in isolation.

The first time I had an orgasm, I thought I was dying. Nobody told me that the room would shake. Creative sexual energy is burning wild. Animals start having sex as soon as their bodies are ready. It's unrealistic to expect that all teenagers can supress their natural hormonal urges.

Sex education addresses bodily changes but should also encompass a teenager's emotional and physical desires. I never lost sleep over my pubic hair, but I lost *plenty* of sleep over *other* boys' pubic hair. The bulk of my crushes, though, were on older men. I knew that made me a faggot. But it didn't occur to me at the time that it made me a gay man.

Rich and I got together several times a week, but our friendship vanished once we started having sex. We no longer talked to each other, because that would require a discussion of sex. Neither of us was ready to have that conversation. Proper sex education would teach young people to have that conversation. Even though he was older than I was, he was also at the beginning of his own coming-out process. In the scheme of things, Rich and I were both babies.

I didn't think of Rich as being gay—he was just a friend with whom I had sex. I wasn't in denial—I just didn't know that having sex with another guy gave me a special identity as a gay man. I didn't know it was an option. The gay men in Lexington were either closeted or frightening grotesques. Danny Lambert was a fortyish man who did yard work for little old ladies in his Daisy Duke cut-off jeans. Schoolboys yelled to Danny just so they could see him wave his hands like a pair of hummingbird wings and shriek, "Hi, boys!" I imagine he was thrilled just to be noticed by so many beautiful children. If anyone was predatory, it was the boys who regarded Danny as their own personal sideshow.

Like most queer kids, I figured it out the hard way—alone, terrified, and confused. Luckily, I was exposed to gay elders who helped me along. I worked it out in the pages of my journal, where I spent hundreds of hours setting down the awkward, embarrassing trajectory of my sexuality.

There were epiphanies along the way, but it's not like I heard Judy Garland's voice and said, "Oh, yeah, I must be *gay*." There was no such watershed. Just when I thought I'd come out, I ended up doing it again and again. Coming-out is never finished.

Straight people always ask "when did you come out?" as if it happened in a single instant. There's no brief or simple answer to that question. Straight people ask such questions like eight-year-olds who want to know every detail about the birthday party to which they weren't invited.

Maybe they envision a secret tribal ceremony that takes place in a faraway land. The forest is so thick that the light of the full moon barely penetrates the branches. Dozens of blindfolded inductees make their way down the forest path, all holding onto a fifty-foot guide rope with both hands. When the blindfolds are removed at midnight, the inductees open their eyes. Before them stand hundreds of villagers, each holding a candle. The flames dance across their naked bodies, throwing reflections onto the glitter paint smeared all over their skin. The villagers start singing in another language. The new villagers join in after only a few lines. It's a song of welcome in a language they all seem to know.

When did you come out?

When I saw the moon.

Wade and Price had come out gradually after I'd told them both I was gay. At that point, they were the only

people I'd told. I was fifteen, but I was further along in the coming-out process than they were. Initially, Wade claimed that he
was bisexual. There are millions of honest-to-goodness bisexu-
als in the world. Wade was not one of them. One night, after our
third beer, I said to him, "You *know* what you think about late
at night." Finally, they'd come out enough to bring me into
Lexington's tiny but growing gay social network.

It was 1988, and we were having a heated discussion around
the pool at Dr. Cabinaw's house. Wade and Edward were argu-
ing in favor of Bush. The rest of us didn't really speak in favor
of Dukakis, so much as against Bush. The Republican party has
a way of tossing plump, stupid birds into the air, to the concomi-
tant delight and chagrin of political skeetshooters everywhere.

Wade was a Republican, which completely baffled me. How does
that happen to gay people? Is it genetic or do they learn it from
their parents? Surely, people don't just pop out of the womb with
an urge to canvass neighborhoods on behalf of people who want
them in prison. A friend said that Jesse Fowler popped out of the
womb screaming "Hand me my brooch!" But that's different.

Dr. Cabinaw was a brilliant man but seemed profoundly uninterested in the particular issues of the race. He wondered aloud

whether one of the Bush cousins was "of the lavender persuasion" or whether Dukakis had ever "left the Sadie Hawkins Dance early." He was like a gay Yoda, speaking in a relentless stream of euphemism.

Edward was half drunk already, ranting patriotically about the virtues of a strong military. Another man, a retired army officer, clinked his glass with a "here, here," even though he was a Democrat. We all knew why Edward was a Republican. Edward was of the species *homo trust fundus*. Dr. Cabinaw referred to him as the "blond angel," despite the fact that he was thirty, pudgy, and still jobless. The two of us shared violent acrimony from the moment we had laid eyes on each other at the record store. Sometimes it took extremely loud music to drown out our battles.

I was bored of fighting and was spacing out, staring across the yard. Sitting on the diving board, I spotted a pickaninny statue. My jaw dropped. I wasn't exactly sure what it was, but I knew it was offensive and I knew I could start a big nasty argument over it. I'd wait and see if the Republican thing died down. The guys from the store had taken me there because these were some of the only homosexuals they'd met in town. It was a rush to meet them, but it was an object lesson as well. Yes, I had one thing in common with these guys, but we also had painful political and generational differences. Sexual identity is powerful common ground to share with another person. But in terms of genuine community, it's water, baby, not blood.

Wade and Price knew them all from school. I think I scared the hell out them, being fifteen and so thoroughly full of myself. Dr. Cabinaw dropped a dazzling flurry of references to gay men throughout history, referring to them as "a bird with violet feathers," "a friend of Dorothy," or "a lover of antiquity." When he ran out of euphemisms, which generally didn't happen until late in the evening, he'd simply say, "He's . . . *ahem* . . . you know."

I'd interrupt him, saying, "Do you mean he's *gay?* Do you mean he fucks *men?*"

Everyone was startled that I'd disrupted his artful indirection.

In some ways, these men were my teachers. And the way I'd always learned the most from my teachers was to spar with them.

It was as if I'd been thrown into the middle of *The Boys in the Band,* and was being forced to trade barbs. Two of them told stories of seeing men at the YMCA in the 1950s. They spoke with great fondness of unrequited crushes. They mythologized college boys around town who were clearly straight. Those stories just made me sad.

One night, we all gathered around the TV set. Dr. Cabinaw had unearthed a video of the classic porn flick *Boys in the Sand.* His collection of pornography was infamous, reputedly occupying a substantial part of his house. That particular video was his favorite, and it was being shown to "educate Master Read in the ways of . . . *ahem* . . . matters of visual artistry."

We were watching Casey Donovan walk out of the surf and up the sand when Wade came running into the living room. He snapped off the TV and turned on the radio. He stifled groans with adamant shushes.

On the radio, a man was talking about being gay. He was British. All huddled around the radio, as if we could get beamed somewhere else if we got close enough. I was curled in a ball on the couch. The radio blared right in my ear. I reached over to turn it up louder.

Wade, the consummate Anglophile, stepped in to translate. "It's Ian McKellen, the Shakespearean actor. He's coming out to protest Section 28 in England."

"What's Section 28?" I asked.

"A law that outlaws promoting homosexuality," Wade said.

"Oh, we must do away with that law," Dr. Cabinaw quipped. "We must promote Greek love at every available opportunity."

The man on the radio spoke with great passion. It was the first time I'd ever heard anyone else come out. He wasn't apologizing or holding anyone's hand. Maybe I would try it that way from then on, the way I'd heard him do it.

When the broadcast was over, no one moved. We all hoped

he would come back on the radio. We sat in silence for about thirty seconds, looking at each other with our eyes open wide. *What just happened was important.*

I found a picture of Ian McKellen at the library and sliced it out of the magazine with an X-Acto knife. I kept the photo in my desk drawer for the rest of high school. Sometimes I talked to him, especially when I was pissed off. Often, I asked him how to be angry and eloquent at the same time.

It was a second marriage for both of us. Shelley

Jansen and I were first married in an intimate ceremony that took place in my backyard. The ring was stolen from my sister, and the bride wore Osh Kosh. We were five.

Our freshman year, we spent every waking moment together. Our class schedules overlapped to the point that some teachers separated us so we wouldn't be disruptive. We shared a brain, pretty much, and everyone knew that if we were huddling up in their vicinity, we were probably trashing them to filth.

We'd reconnected in a small collective of vanquished junior high school politicos. Four girls and I had lost the eighth grade student council elections. We had a losers' party and gave ourselves new identities based on a deck of cards. The girls who'd won the elections were branded the queens of hearts and diamonds, while we reserved for ourselves the purest of suits, the spades. I was the jack, the only face card in our bunch. We loathed queens of all suits and alleviated our disappointment with slumber parties, movie nights, and bitter, get-on-down gossip fests.

By the time we got to high school, Tricia had moved. Johnna was dating a senior, which struck the rest of us as an acute betrayal. We were so pious in our disapproval that we had a sit-down intervention with her mother. But eventually, it passed. Kate split her time between daily dance classes, guy friends, and a startling book-a-day habit.

Shelley and I were alone again.

I'd pretty much grown up at her house. She was the fourth in a large Mormon family. When we were five, her house burned down. When we arrived there from kindergarten, we held hands as the flames engulfed the second story. Her younger sister was stomping her feet, screaming "My *clothes*, my *clothes!*" Shelley cried when her mother drove me home in their Volkswagen bus. She didn't understand why we couldn't play together that day.

Freshman science was taught by a first-year teacher named Mr. Leland. It's safe to say that Shelley and I both became completely obsessed with him, which was a feeling shared by almost everyone in his class.

Mr. Leland cussed in class and drew dazzling colored-chalk murals on the blackboard. He talked honestly about having used drugs. Many of our teachers were baby boomers, but from the way they described their experience of the sixties, it seemed that they had never left their living rooms. Mr. Leland had played in the counterculture's sandbox. In this regard, he was exotic to us. Many of us were experimenting with sex and drugs. Here was someone who was honest about having done the same. In him we caught a glimpse of how we might look on the other side of adolescence. The spectacle was invigorating.

He spouted scientific theories that were several academic years beyond the standard freshman science curriculum. He was altogether different from any teacher we'd ever had before. The boys wanted to be him, the girls wanted to do him, and I wanted a little of each. But what we all had in common—the girls and boys and I—was that we all wanted desperately to be noticed by him, to hold his attention, to impress him. We all wanted to please Mr. Leland.

Johnna had a striking personality conflict with him that resulted in threats of failure, parent-teacher conferences, and shrewd manipulation on her part. Everyone knew she'd pull out an A in the end. For some reason, she had similar clashes with every science teacher she ever had. She's a lawyer now, which means she gets paid for this kind of thing.

Meanwhile, I was failing his class. And by failing, I don't mean I was an overachiever getting his first C. I mean test scores in the low twenties, out of one hundred.

He didn't use a textbook, and we quickly realized that he was teaching us college-level material. His tests and quizzes were bullshit-proof. I was scientifically impaired to begin with. I'd spent my time in junior high school science sitting perilously close to Mason Emore, who drew me into whatever troublesome schemes he'd concocted that day. So, while we were setting rodents free and cracking girls' butts with bandanas, I did not learn much science. I couldn't tell you how to complete an electrical circuit or the difference between a genus and a species.

Mr. Leland let loose his dizzying theories on class field trips to rock outcroppings along Highway 11. I was, without benefit of chemicals, stoned. Shelley was similarly rattled.

There was something very *Dead Poets Society* about that class. As Shelley and I watched and rewatched that movie, searching for ways to break our failing streaks, we both figured we'd end up like the dead actor.

We'd been passing back and forth our obtuse, handwritten philosophical essays. We were reading lots of Og Mandino's Christian self-help novels. Even when we played Super Mario Brothers, we felt we were extremely profound.

We settled on a strategy. Since all of the tests were essays, we'd serve up essays. Neither of us could manage to fill up even a single page about the scientific principles we were supposed to discuss, so we worked them into larger stories. If the question was about volcanic eruptions and the resulting crystalline rock formations, I'd write a long poem about a sputtering Vietnam veteran whose Tourette's syndrome ends up implanting disturbing memories in the brain of everyone within earshot.

Mr. Leland ate it up, and both of us went from failing to As. I fed his mailbox a steady diet of my writing, and he stopped me in the hallway to say "keep it coming." He said little else. He didn't need to. Mr. Leland is, quite simply, the reason I started writing seriously—to pass science.

Shelley and I stayed up until three or four in the morning on weekends, talking on the phone. We had a uniform for such occasions, which consisted of yellow sweatpants and red chamois shirts over R.E.M. tee shirts. We were religious about adhering to this shared wardrobe.

We spent every lunch period together, holed up in the audio-visual room. We gorged on Diet Cokes and Cheez-Its, which was our version of a monk's diet. We talked endlessly of Mr. Leland, trying to conceal the fact that we were competitive about the attention we each received.

Everyone assumed that Shelley and I were an item, in that simplistic "men and women can't be just friends" kind of way. Truth was, we were both completely crushed out over a pair of Mormon missionaries. All the boys with nametags wound up in pairs at the Jansen house. Pairs of Mormon missionaries never split up lest one of them succumb to wicked sin, like caffeine. They came to the Jansen house for video games and food. Someone is always making English muffin pizzas in a Mormon household. *Always.*

I met Elder Hobbs at Shelley's house and promptly fell for him. Shelley liked his missionary partner, which made our dual infatuations especially convenient. I went to their church just to be around Elder Hobbs and even considered becoming Mormon.

I loved the way Shelley's family interacted. They had meetings and ate meals together and went to each other's piano recitals. They didn't appear the least bit fractured. My family was nothing if not fractured.

To our dismay, Elder Hobbs's and his partner's two-year mission came to an end. He didn't convert me, but he sure distracted me.

So I set my sights on someone closer to home—Robin Massie, a star of the LHS girls varsity basketball team. Shelley played basketball, which meant that I attended all of her games, whether they were at home or on the road.

All that exposure to athletics must have recruited me temporarily into the heterosexual lifestyle, because I developed a painful case of hormones for a girl.

Robin was a senior and we were freshmen. She didn't walk, she swaggered—to the point that sometimes I'd wonder if some sports-related injury was the cause of her deliciously slow mosey through our high school hallways. But no, child, it was hormonal. She was butcher than all the men I've ever dated put together.

Her locker was eleven doors down from mine. I'd sneak glances of her as she went about her morning routine. First, she'd set her duffel bag on the floor. Then she'd put her red down vest on the coat hook. It was the sort of vest you'd wear while hunting deer.

Then she'd look in the mirror and primp her hair, which was the classic girl-jock hairdo: bangs in front, feathered on the sides, long and scraggly in back. She looked like a hockey player with teeth or a heavy metal guitarist without hairspray. It was enough to cause my forehead to bead up with sweat. When she styled her hair, she did it with her fingers—nails bitten to the quick—without a hairbrush in sight. I never talked to her, but I wanted her.

One day I dug through my father's closet and found a pair of cowboy boots. Dad and I wore all the same sizes, so I was in luck. I wore them to school, completely mortified every time the heels clicked on the linoleum floor of those hallowed halls. I might as well have been wearing Manolo Blahnik pumps. Those Naugahyde, machine-tooled, made-in-China booties were not making me the least bit butcher.

All of my self-consciousness was justified when Shelley brought me a tiny folded note. Shelley said, "Let's duck into a sound-proof room." A wise move, I would soon realize.

There, in tightly wrought cursive, were the words "Kirk—You look good in them boots.—Robin." I squealed, jumping up and down on the teacher's desk until the vice-principal walked in and asked, "Aren't you two supposed to be in class?"

Shelley squinted at him, took a long sip of Diet Coke, and said, "Probably."

I did all of my freshmen algebra homework while logging assists and fouls for the girls varsity basketball team. I was in heat every time Robin fouled out or mouthed off at a ref.

When Robin's birthday rolled around, Shelley scored party invitations for both of us. The party was held at the Rockbridge County Recreational Center. Throughout the evening, Shelley and I downed cheap keg beer, wine coolers, shots—anything that was handed to us. I felt it was my duty to drink screwdrivers, because I'd discovered that they were Robin's favorite drink. That was the night Shelley and I learned about mixing drinks in one's stomach.

Shelley and I, both dance-shy, entered the zone commonly known in Rockbridge County as *all tore up*. We stumbled onto the dance floor. Robin and her boyfriend Cecil were dancing a few couples away. Cecil was twenty-something and had a moustache, which Shelley and I found shocking. Cecil was the sort of guy whose mere shove could have put me in the hospital. So I kept at ten paces—close enough for yearning, far enough for safety.

At the end of the evening, Shelley's brother gave us a ride home. He was dating Robin's sister, so we drove to Robin's house. While he was inside kissing her good night, I reached out of the car's open door and filled the pockets of my overcoat with gravel from Robin's driveway. I then proceeded to vomit out the door. I was still puking when Shelley's brother returned and pulled back on the road.

When I got home, I tripped up the steps and collapsed on my bed. The room was spinning. I'd left my clothes up and down the hallway and was now in underwear and a Dead Kennedys tee shirt.

The Colonel appeared at my bedside and said, "Goddamn it, boy. You've been drinking." He made an attempt to blame the entire incident on the Mormons, and I was far too drunk for a rebuttal.

I didn't convince him of my sobriety, but I did talk him into letting me go to sleep. Then came a beautiful and angelic voice: "You feel yucky, don't you?"

I melted and said, "Yes, Mommy. I feel yucky."

"Goddamn it, boy," growled my father, whom I'd forgotten about altogether. Dad flicked on the lights and shook a handful of gravel in my face.

"What in the hell is this?" he bellowed.

"It's gravel, Colonel. And it's too long a story to tell right now."

Shelley and I both were grounded, but somehow we managed to convince our parents that being grounded didn't preclude spending time with one another.

The next night, we cranked my stereo and climbed out onto the roof. We had albums in common, naturally. Our favorite was *Eagles Live*, which we'd play as we gazed into the night sky. The stars, we reasoned, were concertgoers, each holding a butane lighter. As far as we were concerned, all those people were there to see us.

I'd known Eve Hill since I was a wee tot. My mother's

housekeeper, Burmah, babysat me when my parents went out of town. This meant I got to play with her daughter, Matie, and some of the other kids on Diamond Hill, the black neighborhood in Lexington. I should clarify—I got to play with the black *girls* on Diamond Hill.

I was so jealous. They all had fabulous nicknames like "Puddin'" and "Boobie" and "Naynay." I'd wanted a nickname so much that in kindergarten I had started calling myself "Flash." It didn't work at all.

Some of their parents played music out their windows. Sometimes we'd dance to albums they seemed to know by heart—Stevie Wonder, Chaka Khan, the Jackson Five. My father played Benny Goodman and Glenn Miller. I was getting ripped off.

At first they giggled at me because I'd never really danced before. Then I watched them. They rolled their hips around, closed their eyes, and rocked their shoulders from side to side. Maybe boys were supposed to do it differently, but they were the only teachers I had. So I threw my hips around just like Matie and her friends.

We played kickball, hide-and-seek, and dressed up Matie's black and white Barbies. I was shaking with excitement. I'd never played with dolls, let alone black ones. Black Barbie was bigger than White Barbie. Matie grabbed them at one point and knocked them against each other. She made them talk.

BLACK BARBIE: I'm bigger than you.
WHITE BARBIE: Please don't hurt me!
BLACK BARBIE: Take that!
WHITE BARBIE: No!

I was so enthralled with the two Barbies that I didn't even bother with Ken. Barbie had better clothes, so who cared about Ken? None of White Barbie's clothes fit Black Barbie, so you had to stretch them onto Black Barbie and it always looked wrong. Matie and her friends left the room to ask Burmah for candy money, and I stayed in the room with my new friends. They scored a few quarters and asked me if I wanted to go with them.

"No," I said. "I'll stay here."

I combed Black Barbie's hair for ten solid minutes. I'd watched in amazement as Burmah combed her own hair in the mirror. It was completely different from the way my mother combed hers. When I was alone in Burmah's bathroom, I ran one of those combs through my hair. It left a slightly greasy residue. I touched the teeth of the comb, then rubbed my thumb against the rest of my fingers.

I worried that I'd be caught playing with her comb, but my hair was sweaty anyway. The heat in the house was tropical on account of Burmah's elderly aunt living there. I hardly ever saw Matie's father. I just thought he worked all the time. I didn't know what divorce was then.

I sat the Barbies on the edge of the bed and dressed them. Their hands fit together. I put bows in their hair and dressed them in the prettiest skirts and blouses I could find. I walked them all over the carpet, holding hands.

Matie burst into the room and shut the door.

"Didja fight 'em?" she asked, then dropped her voice to a whisper. "Didja make 'em do *nasty* things?"

"No," I said, pointing at the two Barbies, sitting on the edge of the bed, hands touching. "They're best friends."

Eve and Wanda and Theresa and a bunch of other black girls were gathered around Jesse in the middle of the gym floor. I was in ninth grade and this was my first high school sock hop. They were dancing hard to Prince's "Let's Go Crazy." We'd all memorized the spoken introduction: *Dearly beloved, we are gathered here today to get through this thing called life.*

Jesse could dance like no one at our school. The black girls were constantly telling him he had too much soul to be a white boy. I desperately wanted them to say that to me. I danced about twenty feet from them. Jesse brought out moves that had the girls clapping and stomping.

After watching them for half an hour, I realized what was going on. They taught Jesse how to move his hips and head. Jesse taught them how to bring their arms into it. As I looked around the gym at all the white kids dancing, I thought about how badly our school needed these lessons.

Lesson Number One: If you're white, do not snap your fingers while music is playing. It looks silly. It's one of the things only a black person can get away with, like carrying an oversized comb in the back pocket. Do not attempt if white.

Lesson Number Two: If you're black, you don't have to move much on the dance floor. A white person has to do all this extra stuff, spinning and clapping and whatnot. A black person can barely be moving and you just *get* that they're dancing.

A Depeche Mode song came on and Jesse led the dance. He did this thing with his arms where he pushed all the way out with both hands, then pulled one fist back all the way and leaned his head back. I could hear the girls chanting "Go Jesse! Go Jesse! Go Jesse!"

Someday, I hoped, they would say my name on the dance floor, just like that.

"Ooh, *child*," I said to Eve, who turned her face to me in mock defiance of the gym teacher who strode past us.

Eve and I often shared sick-note afternoons in last period ninth-grade gym. We pretended to do our homework but spent the entire period gossiping. Eve didn't even bother to fake it. I'd at least have a book open on my knees, in the event that our gym teacher passed.

Eve and the two gym teachers were black, so Eve knew instinctively how to get her way. She didn't get special treatment, but those women knew there were days you just didn't mess with Eve. White teachers who lacked such insight were often sorry later.

Eve was scary when she needed to be. Growing up I'd always loved her braids because she had those ponytail ties with marble-sized crystal balls. I always wanted to touch them to see what sort of sound they made when two of them clinked together. But even in second grade, I knew that there were things in this world that were simply off-limits—a white boy touching a black girl's hair without invitation, for instance.

Ms. Turrell, one of the gym teachers, walked by again. I grabbed my textbook and pretended to read.

"I can see what you're up to, Kirk," she said.

Eve didn't bother to reach for her book. She even removed a bottle of nail polish from her purse and started to unscrew it.

"*Child!*" I said.

"Yes, indeed," Eve said, sticking her middle finger in the air. "Y'mama's chipped."

I tried to get some bass in my voice so I'd sound more like her. Eve coached me.

Eve and I never talked about my being gay, not explicitly, anyway. But she knew. One doesn't make a straight boy rehearse saying "Ooo, *child*," does one? Eve armed me with the attitude I'd need to protect myself. She had been doing just that for years.

"Ooo, *child*," I said, snapping my neck from side to side.

Eve exploded into giggles.

"Thass right!" she said, rolling her head in front of her slowly.

It's all about chin, neck, and lips, I realized. Those are the parts that do the real rolling. I tried again.

"Ooo, *child*," I said, then added three snaps and a quick roll of my eyes. Eve loved that.

"See!" she said, an octave below her speaking voice.

"Mmmmm," I replied, in a bass voice that barely left my throat.

Finally, I put my algebra book into my backpack and zipped it up. If Ms. Turrell came by again, she'd just have to deal me.

sex on a school night

The apartment was dark, except for the light from the street lamps outside his bedroom window.
It spilled through the edges of the downturned blinds and dropped rows of light on our skin. They were skeletal, like ribs.

Rich picked up a condom from the windowsill. His hands were shaking, so he tore open the foil packet with his teeth. He put on a condom and rubbed KY on his dick. I kneeled on the edge of the bed so he could stand behind me. And then I waited. I'd been practicing for this moment for a long time but Rich didn't know that. He was scared he would hurt me and wanted to go slow.

I'd never used KY before. It was sticky, like warm molasses. I'd used virtually everything in my house as lube. Every time my parents left for a cocktail party, I'd dash into their bathroom for a different potion. I used conditioner, Jergen's lotion, Oil of Olay, Mary Kay night cream, Vaseline, baby oil.

"You're not gonna hurt me," I said.

Rich pushed gently and was surprised when he slid all the way in without me screaming.

"Are you okay?" he asked.

"Yeah, I'm fine," I said.

I closed my eyes and watched the movie in my head. Algebra homework, empty beer cans. I saw Rock Hudson in a wheelchair with crossbones through his head. I heard kids screaming "Roll AIDS" and then a laugh track from a sitcom.

"Are you sure you're okay?" Rich asked.

"It doesn't hurt at all," I said.

I thought it would be more of a challenge, even though I had been practicing.

Rich started moving faster inside me. It didn't occur to me to stroke my own dick. I just waited for him to finish, because I thought that was what I was supposed to do. It didn't take him long.

When he pulled out, I spun around to face him.

"I want to see it," I said, removing the condom and holding it close to my face. The end was full of semen, and I pinched it to see how it would move.

"Are you okay?" Rich asked again. He must have been terrified.

"Let's do it again," I said. "I want to go again."

vivisection

Coach Edwards and I did not care for one another.

He was my sophomore biology teacher, and he had the distinction of being the sole male coach/teacher for whom I didn't pen thinly or not-so-thinly veiled love poems. We were both better off for the brief disruption in this romantic pattern.

First, there was the matter of his attire, which was *way* khaki. I was in my tie dye-rock band-baggy pants phase. So, even with our many other differences aside, we were engaged in a bitter war of textiles.

His class was basically pure memorization, a marked change from Mr. Leland. Coach Edwards read through notes on his overhead projector in outline form. I grew to loathe Roman numerals that year. The tests were multiple choice regurgitations of the class notes he pulled from his files year after year. If you studied, you were assured an easy A.

He was a by-the-book kind of disciplinarian, which meant that he recorded tardiness in his grade book using red hatch marks. I was chronically late to all my classes. Five minutes was not enough time for proper hallway schmoozing. Most teachers understood that.

Upon my third late appearance, Coach Edwards sent me to STOP, which stands for Student Time-Out Place. At first I thought he was joking. When he pointed me toward the hallway, I rolled my eyes and said, "Oh, come *on*." He turned bright red and said, "Get out."

This was during the first week of class. So from the get-go there was no love lost between this man and me. He represented everything that was evil: misguided machismo, junior varsity athletics, and flagrant heterosexuality. I'd have racked up tardies just to stay out of his class altogether, except that the next step was in-school suspension. That would go on the permanent record. That would require parental signatures. In-school suspension was not the power move.

I was a smart-ass who voiced suspicion about the way teachers treated athletes. He was riding school buses with these boys to away games in counties I'd never even heard of. That sort of male bonding, I reasoned, was exactly why I got sent to STOP while others exchanged warm daily sports anecdotes with the coach. I had no such anecdotes.

He was further annoyed by the fact that I'd miss entire days of school to see out-of-town concerts. He didn't know I was going with Rich, but his warped little imagination probably cooked up a far more sinister explanation for my whereabouts. He knew I was queer and the tension that that caused was palpable.

When we covered human sexuality, he used the blackboard instead of the overhead projector. Bless his heart, the lesson plan had him so nervous that his voice was shaking. He wrote the word *homosexuality* on the board and sheepishly explained what in the hell that is. He calmly shushed a few groans and gags from the class.

As soon as he quieted them, I swear to God, he looked at me—and it wasn't one of the mean, accusatory looks he gave me on a daily basis. I think he was checking on me. As he trudged through a thankfully brief rundown on homosexuality, I held my breath. I was trying to decide whether to crawl under my desk or to jump up on the lab table and tell everyone to stop snickering at who I was. His definition was very clinical, and it sounded nothing like the homosexuality I was getting every chance I could. It sounded nothing like the homosexuality I'd had up my butt the night before.

Apart from the words *homosexuality* and *same sex*, he didn't write much down. This meant it wasn't going to show up on the test. Which was a shame, because I could have written that man one burning hell of an extra-credit essay.

I doodled in my notebook and wrote snippets of poems all period. I couldn't look up for the rest of class. Hearing my classmates cluck and giggle at words such as *vulva* and *epididymis* was disheartening. How could I come all the way out when teachers treated it like some sort of tragic affliction?

An English teacher, talking about Hemingway, broached "the gay issue" this way: "There are some scholars who say that Hemingway was . . . questioning . . . his . . . manhood." She paused dramatically, then squeezed a tissue in her left hand. Teachers' shame directly affected the way students reacted to mentions of homosexuality. If teachers could have just been matter-of-fact about it, fewer people would have tittered. But it's not as if anyone taught the teachers how to approach the subject.

Spring is the harvest for biology students. We were required to dissect fish, which was simply not possible for me. The smell of fish completely works me into a dither. I think I might be allergic. I can't even be in the same room as a plate of sushi without feeling a pull in my stomach. So I did what any normal budding radical queer would do: I became an avid animal rights activist. (It should be known that during this period, my favorite meal was a chicken fillet sandwich from Wendy's. Nobody's perfect.)

During ninth grade, I'd discovered People for the Ethical Treatment of Animals because they released a compilation of interesting music called *Animal Liberation*. Inside the album cover,

I found PETA literature and a merchandise order form. I ordered a caged monkey tee shirt and covered my locker with gory pictures of vivisection sure to offend everyone who saw them. Locker decorations of any sort were against school rules, so this was doubly naughty. Understand that there was no Vietnam for my generation. Nobody gave a shit about anything. I was at least *trying*.

I wore the PETA shirt to class repeatedly just to get a rise out of Coach Edwards. When I broke the news to him that I wouldn't be dissecting a fish, which I named Henry, he tried to talk me out of my protest. He wanted me to watch as my lab partner dissected the fish. I refused to be in the room while it was going on, *period*. I told him I wouldn't be *part of the system*—I actually used that phrase. All of this occurred in front of the entire class.

He turned bright red again, like the day he sent me to STOP, then told me to see him after class. He gave me diagrams of a fish to memorize. When D-day arrived, he pushed a desk into the hallway and said I was to sit there all period.

"Can't I go to the library?" I asked.

"No," he said.

"People sit in the hall when they get kicked out of class."

"You're just going to have to sit there," he said.

I gritted my teeth and growled at him as I sat down with my fish diagram. During that hour, I read from Peter Singer's book *Animal Liberation*, hoping that Coach Edwards would walk out to find me straying from his orders. He never did.

Several weeks later, we had to dissect frogs in class. I got far more uppity.

"Why do we have to dissect frogs?" I asked.

"Because it will help you see where the organs are," Coach Edwards replied.

"What if we don't care where the organs are?"

"It's in case you go into the medical profession."

"If I don't want to slice up a frog, why would I want to slice up a human?"

"Don't get smart."

"Why can't you just do *one* as a demonstration?"

"Because the state requires that I do it this way."

"Well, the state is *wrong*."

"I take it you're going to continue your little protest."

"You got that right, *coach*."

He glared at me. "You watch that attitude, young man."

I looked down at my arms and legs, pretending to watch my attitude. He made the *ah-ah* sound that parents make when you're about to get bitch-slapped.

The day the frogs arrived, the hall reeked of formaldehyde. Again, I sat in the hallway while my classmates sliced up dead frogs which were raised by the thousands for just this purpose.

That day I wrote down everything I saw in the hallway. I saw exasperated teachers stepping outside for a sanity check. I saw exiled students sitting alone. We waved to each other, like we were fellow inmates. I didn't want them to know that I was only engaging in a frog-in. I wanted them to think I'd been kicked out like they had. This place where I was sitting—this was where outlaws sat.

I didn't study the frog diagram very thoroughly and got a C, which I shined on. I didn't even give Coach Edwards the satisfaction of an indignant response. As he handed me the graded test, I flashed him a toothy grin and stuffed the paper into my notebook without looking at it.

Coach Edwards and I exchanged one last aggressive stare before the bell rang. Being an outlaw was going to be one hell of a lot of fun.

I would not be on board for the second year of this class, which involved slicing up fetal pigs. I was learning all I ever wanted to know about biology on field trips to Rich's house.

Coach Philips was a five-foot version of Tom Selleck.
He was one of those coaching squad people who is shoehorned into academia against the better judgment of all involved parties.

Half the year we spent in P.E., which required us to wear thoroughly degrading red polyester shorts. I frequently received numeric penalties when my boxers poked out below my shorts. I was not a briefs kind of teenager and I was roundly punished for it. The second half of the year was spent in driver's education.

Instead of teaching, Coach Philips frequently rented relevant movies such as *Summer School.* This was probably for the best. He was a male chauvinist nightmare. He flirted overtly with girls, made condescending remarks to me for not playing a "real" sport, and scrutinized like an IRS auditor every sick-note that crossed his desk.

Predictably, I fell madly in love with him.

I went to great lengths to schedule gym last period, so I wouldn't have to shower in that moldy, dilapidated locker room. Sophomore year, I dropped world history just to avoid having gym third period. Much has been made in gay porn of the high school shower scene. But when you're in the moment, the prospect of showering alongside rapidly developing boys sparks acute terror.

Seniors shared the gym with us last period. Gym was only required for two years, so the folks who signed up for it as an elective belonged to some bizarre sect of career P.E. students. The boys from that class did their best to intimidate the rest of us, nabbing plum lockers and shooting dirty looks if we took up too much space while dressing.

Shalewa refused to remove her jewelry in gym. She too lost points. During inspection, Coach Philips would peer over his clipboard at Shalewa's many stud earrings, which outlined her lobes like centipedes.

"You know I'm going to dock you for those."

"Mmmm-hmmmm," Shalewa would say, scratching at her scalp with a substantial fingernail. Then she'd lean her head back and say something utterly X-rated in a whisper that was intended for me. Shalewa's whispers always went well beyond the person she was addressing.

We sat next to each other during driver's ed and passed notes all period. My favorite days were Mondays, when she would reveal the utterly filthy things she'd done that weekend. Coach Philips intercepted several of our notes, threatening to read them aloud, then realized that such a disciplinary measure could easily cost him his job.

She spent a lot of time in STOP. This did not seem to scare her. At the mere mention of STOP, many kids would squirm in their seats, visualizing large black marks being burned into their transcript. Shalewa just took it as a provocation.

The first week of first grade, Shalewa had gotten a spanking with a paddle with holes in it. Schoolyard legend had it that the paddle left oozing, bloody blisters on the rumps of misbehaving children. We all heard Shalewa's paddling, two doors down. It was the first time I heard her voice. It was also the first time I heard the word *bitch*. Shalewa said it between whacks.

I let her read my poems to Coach Philips, though I didn't tell her who'd inspired them. "You're after *some*thing," she said.

"That comes across?" I asked.

"Baby, it's all out there," she said.

I slipped a steady stream of poems under Coach Philips's office door. I'd sneak into the locker room after school, when all the lights were out. I put them in an envelope bearing his name, then pushed them into his six-by-eight-foot office.

It usually took him a few days to acknowledge a poem. He'd call me up to his desk and tell me it was good but that he didn't understand all of it. This, of course, was not his fault. If you're averaging fifteen metaphors per page, you need a good hard slap.

One day, Coach Philips was trying to calm down the class. The football team had lost a key game the night before, and he was grouchy.

"I want total silence. If anyone speaks, they'll get a zero for the day."

A single zero could bring one's six-week grade down an entire letter. College-obsessed children had done this math before. Shalewa didn't give a rat's ass and kept poking me with her pornographic confessions.

"Shhh," I whispered. "A zero is *really* bad."

Coach Philips stood up and wiggled his Napoleonic little frame over to my desk.

"Zero!" he said. "And you're going to STOP."

"But I was just trying to . . ."

"She can take care of herself."

"*That's* fucked up," Shalewa said. Everyone gasped.

Shalewa and I sat in STOP together for three long afternoons, unable to talk because of the partitions. Some teachers let us watch soap operas and eat candy in STOP. But lucky us, we got Ms. Hostetter, who seemed to regard her gestapo role as a divine calling. The last day of our purgatory, we swapped yearbooks under the partitions and asked for inscriptions.

Neither of us had finished the six-question contracts that were required in STOP. Questions included "What did you do?", "Did your behavior help you to be successful in school?", and "What are three acceptable consequences if you break this contract?"

As I was trying to feign remorse, Shalewa slid my yearbook back to me. In it she'd written

Kirk,

My French is terrible so I'm not going to even try to write any.

We have two more years to go. Can we stand it?

We have known each other since kindergarten. (Is that spelled right?)

Good luck with whatever you do and whoever you do it with.

Don't ever change.

Yours truly,

Shalewa

Now *that's* poetry.

The worst fears of radical right wingers are well-founded.

It only takes one or two lefties in a place to radicalize the children. Kimberly Tuccione was our fifty-something, four-foot-eleven librarian who proved that Lexington's lily-white Protestants couldn't tell the difference between pushy Italian and pushy Jew. She was brash was all they could figure. Ms. Tucci loved kids to the point that she was annoying. Just when I least expected it, she'd scuffle over with something that I *must* read. On days when I was not up for her, I wouldn't walk past the library.

She'd show up at every cultural event in town. People saw her coming and quickly walked away, knowing they were about to get mauled by La Tucci. She loved getting up in my face to tell me what to do. Once, when I was at a folk concert, she cornered me and said, "You have to promise me you'll see the film *Jean de Florette*. You'll *hate* it but at least we can talk about it."

She nagged me for weeks on end when Nat Hentoff was coming to town. We sat together during his lecture about the First Amendment. She clutched her heart and swooned the entire time.

When John Updike came to the chapel at W&L, Ms. Tucci taped reminder notes for me outside Latin class. He read his poetry, which Ms. Tucci later denounced as "doggerel." He read a ridiculous satire of political correctness with a character named Multi Culti. It was good to see a famous writer bomb.

Ms. Tucci always encouraged me to "write for the whole damn world." She told me to *never, ever* be a Southern writer.

"What do you know from shtupping sheep?" she asked.

When Charles Reagan Wilson's and William Ferris's *Encyclopedia of Southern Culture* was published, she pulled it out of the shipping box with a pained look on her face. "*Southern culture,*" she scoffed. "That's an oxymoron."

When I was fourteen, Ms. Tucci gave me articles she'd clipped from the *Utne Reader* and *Mother Jones.* Because of her, our school library even had a subscription to the *Village Voice* and she demanded that I take home back issues. Ms. Tucci made notes in the margins about each article and circled important bands that were playing at the Knitting Factory.

The *Village Voice* astounded me. Every Tuesday, Ms. Tucci got the latest issue in the mail and gave me the old one to take home. I'd go home and wonder if I could ever be as smugly intelligent as those folks. I imagined that they all worked in a huge room together. Surely, they smoked each other's cigarettes and had rage-filled conversations about spanking and socialism.

Michael Feingold, the theater critic, became an imaginary gay uncle. In a column in which he reviewed five or six plays, he averaged a dozen references to other plays and books. I made lists, then checked out all of those books I could find. Those columns offered much comfort to a faraway theater lover.

I wrote letters to some of the men in the *Voice*'s personal ads. Most didn't respond, either because I wasn't in New York or, more likely, because I was a teenager. Eventually, I ended letters by writing "Please write back to me. *Please.*" It never occurred to me to be afraid of predators. Some wrote back letters that read, essentially, "Hang in there. I can't write to you because I'm scared of being arrested." They probably felt like they'd received a letter from a prison inmate. I was locked up, far away, and wasn't due to be released for some time. A few, however, are still friends and pen pals.

Adults have a responsibility to be visible and available to young gay people. Access to adult worlds, especially those of gay adults, kept me from becoming a suicide statistic. We're separated by cultural terror. My relationships with adult gay people, sexual as well as platonic, knocked a solid ten years off the time it takes many people to come out. Young people desperately need mentors apart from the airbrushed celebutantes they're fed by TV. Sexual awareness *must* be a natural part of puberty.

"*POO-berty*," Ms. Tuccione always insisted. "It's pronounced *POO-berty*."

I'd been up until 4:30 A. M. writing and wasn't budging.

It was 9:20, which meant I had twenty-five minutes to shower, dress, and drive to school. I'd built myself a morning cushion by scheduling an independent study first period. Since I was nocturnal, this was helpful. I tried for a second-period double feature, but even with an understanding guidance counselor, there were limits.

"You need Algebra II," she told me.

"Like I need chemotherapy," I replied.

She won, and Mrs. Brewbaker was thoroughly delighted to have my chronically late, sleepy, and petulant rear end in her class. I sat in the front row to facilitate easy post-bell slip-ins.

"So happy you could join us," she'd chirp, buzzing on coffee and cigarettes—then undeveloped habits which might have made me more tolerable to some teachers.

My study hall proctor knew that I slept through first period because I wrote late at night. My name was on her class roll only as a formality. I missed the absolute legal limit of days in school, but received perfect attendance because the proctor marked me present by default. In a sweet moment of irony, it was Mrs. Brewbaker who had to hand me that certificate at the awards ceremony.

When the bell rang, I bolted out the door. As usual, my backpack weighed around thirty pounds. I carried all of my books so I wouldn't have to visit my locker between classes. I'd started using both shoulder straps because of a paper Shelley had written in Mr. Leland's class on the principle of isostasy. When the Earth's crust sinks in one place, equilibrium demands that somewhere else, land rises. Plus, using both straps hurt less, which is as good a reason as any for change.

I got a long drink of water, then used my shirt sleeve to wipe the dribble from my mouth. The overhead lights in the hallway were flickering slightly. Lockers were slamming like a trash can symphony. I walked up the stairs, past the library, and past the bulletin board where my English teacher let me post a dozen of my poems. I'd mounted them on torn pieces of construction paper, which she said was an old teacher's trick. There, in dot matrix print, were my tortured musings for all the world to see. There were enough icky abstractions that anyone who wasn't meant to get it wouldn't.

We were about three minutes into the break between second and third periods, and I was thinking about lunch. I was wondering if Evan Wyatt knew I had a crush on him. I was hoping Ms. Jenkins wouldn't hand back our Latin tests that day, despite the fact that she graded tests faster than any teacher in the entire school.

Carrie Shiftlett was Frenching Darryl Knick, Mr. Grody was walking toward them to break it up, and Anthony Crevello, who everyone thought was satanic, was banging his acne-covered forehead against his locker door.

I was ten paces from my class when I felt a tug on my backpack. I turned my head to see who it was and got pulled back five feet. My feet left the floor. The pack came off in his hand. When I landed, I fell back into him, which only seemed to make him angrier. He pushed my face up against the air vents on the locker. My lip rested on one of the edges of the vent. I knew if he pressed up, there would be blood.

"You a fuckin' queer?" he asked.

It was Cameron Mills, and he was choking me. I wriggled, then felt him clamp down on my wrists as he pulled my arms behind my back.

"I said, you a fuckin' queer?"

"Yes," I said.

He choked me with his other hand and put his knee against the small of my back. He pushed me into the locker.

"I'll kill ya," he said.

I looked up through the vents in the locker. Straight up, I could see the ceiling out of my left eye. I floated there.

The bell rang and I pushed back against him with all my might. I glared at him, wanting desperately to think of a fitting zinger to suck all the air out of the hallway. He held his fist to the side of my head and grunted. I kept staring. He shook his fist like he was going to hit me, then backed off. He gave my backpack a hard kick, sending it across the hall.

I straightened my shirt and neatened up my hair as best I could. As I retrieved my backpack, I looked up at a teacher who'd seen the attack.

My eyes asked, "Why didn't you do anything?"

She looked away toward her classroom, then shut the door. It was the first time I'd ever seen that teacher shut her door.

I was late for Latin. Ms. Jenkins shot me an imperious look and asked me to translate as soon as I sat down.

Latin spawned an entire subculture at our school. I took it for five years, and my free time was frequently occupied by Roman banquets, Latin club activities, and pseudo-hazing rituals for inductees into our honor society. Latin class was well known as a safe place for freaks, geeks, and budding queer kids. But that day, the very notion of safety seemed as dead as the language we were unraveling.

For the remainder of class, I doodled in the margins of my notebook. I drew stars and patterns, because I didn't know how to draw anything else.

As I entered my next class, I threw my backpack against the

concrete wall and yelled "Shit!" I brooded through the entire class, which was okay because it was English and Ms. Curtis was accustomed to my brooding.

After class, she sat down in the seat in front of me and asked what was wrong.

"Nothing," I said, copping an attitude she didn't deserve.

"You come in here, you throw your satchel against the wall, you say 'Shit' and do Angry Young Man all period."

I told her I was sorry, then walked downstairs, past the office, past the cafeteria, and out the front door.

I started my car, and headed for the river. I went to the place I always went to for quiet. It was down a steep hillside that was blanketed in poison oak. I always slipped at least twice on spots made slippery by pine needles. At the river, there was a long wall made of limestone and a series of smooth places to sit. I'd made up stories about how the wall got there, all of them involving floods and ghosts who held back the river with their breath.

Cameron had just lost his father in a car accident. His brother had given me a beer once. His sister was disarmingly sweet. Half the faculty went to his father's funeral. I didn't want to get him in trouble. Nothing would have happened anyway.

Three years later, I would understand the rage of losing a father too soon. I would understand the desire to put your fingers around the neck of someone who still had a father and squeeze.

At the time, I was pissed he'd made me late for class. I didn't understand how he could attack me in front of twenty people and none of them could be bothered to stop. And I couldn't stop seeing that teacher's door close.

Boys will be boys and hurt boys will hurt boys—that's what I figured I'd hear. Did I really need to hear that directly from the vice principal's mouth?

I hadn't cried, and I was proud of that. I wasn't going to let him make me cry. I wrote down a steady stream of horrible phrases to describe him. I tried to cheer myself by writing out his nasty fate—welfare, dirty babies, grueling construction work. It just made me feel like a nasty snob, and two hours later I was still quaking.

I put down my notebook and looked out across the river. On the other side, a cow was wading into the current. It slowed down where the pull of the rapids got strong. The cow turned until it was facing directly against the current, its head inches above the surface. Then it just stood there. It was a contest to see which was heavier, the river or the cow itself. After ten minutes, the cow had stood its ground and won. The cow climbed the bank and returned to the meadow where it gnawed at tall grass. Ten minutes—one stubborn cow.

houseguests

Just because I was born Southern does not mean that I was born a gracious host. Like most attributes, party-giving is a learned behavior, despite the genetic assistance afforded by my compulsively social parents. My first attempt to throw a large gathering for wayward teenagers was an unmitigated disaster.

Valerie and I attended our sophomore homecoming together so that we could both avoid the parliamentary procedure of dating. This was the first of many instances in which I was a sought-after date because I was "fun, with no sexual hassles." She was unexpectedly demure in a floral-print cotton dress, no doubt selected by her mother. She drove, all the while flicking cigarette ashes out the window and cranking the Doors loud enough to cause inner-ear trauma.

I was pure thrift shop, wearing lots of browns and earthy greens. Together, the two of us resembled a blossoming compost pile. The dance itself went well enough. My parents had a houseguest who was in her eighties, so they approached my throwing an after-party at our house with mild trepidation.

"Honey," my mother leveled with me, "at 2 A. M., I'm calling the police. That's how I broke up the parties your brother and sister had."

That way, she reasoned, I wouldn't have to tell people to go home. It would also bestow legendary status upon the party. High schoolers quickly forget whether they had a good time at a particular party, but if spinning blue lights are required to bring a party to conclusion, it's a success. In a small town, the whole purpose of a party is to provide excitement that the environment lacks. When a town is small enough to have a part-time mayor, this often takes the form of spray painting water towers, stealing flowers from graves, and having a police officer misspell your name in his little spiral notebook.

Valerie and I left the dance early to set up the party. By the time we got home, there were about a dozen people in my backyard, mostly guys I'd never met from other high schools. My father was already pacing.

"I told those boys there would be no drinking," Dad said, having finished his three scotches of the evening.

"Colonel, don't talk to anyone else, okay?"

"It's my house, goddamn it. I don't want *drinking* here."

Mom intervened and sent me back outside. Our houseguest looked up from the kitchen table and said, "Is there something wrong with the backyard?"

I'd gone about party preparations all wrong. I'd bought lots of soda and snacks, but had no alcohol to serve. Parties were usually BYOB anyway, and since I was fifteen, this really couldn't be helped.

I'd made mixed tapes that would set the mood and take us from 9 P. M. to 3 A. M. I made the tapes with the best of intentions, figuring I would bring bands like Let's Active and Hüsker Dü to the ears of Lexington High School. The boys in my backyard were already playing Lynyrd Skynyrd they'd retrieved from their trucks.

I might as well call the police now, I figured. This party has already gotten away from me.

I was a paranoid bitch from the moment I arrived, motioning people not to dance in flower beds or do pull-ups on the grape arbors. These are not behaviors that should require a host's admonishment in the first place. But when you throw a party without written invitations, you are begging for guests bereft of social graces. You are inviting strangers into your home, but you are not inviting their manners.

The yard and our guesthouse filled up with close to a hundred people, all told. Several of my friends could tell I was already sour on the party and encouraged me to relax. I changed the music, took deep breaths, and ate some of the pretzels which otherwise had gone untouched. People just wanted a place to drink, basically.

Kate was holding my hands and talking me down when I heard the words *faggot* and *homo* ring through the yard.

"That's it," I said, rifling through the kitchen drawers for a deterrent. I grabbed a hammer and sped out the door. Half my friends were laughing, the other half covered their mouths or sang my name with the music of concern.

Outside, two boys were tussling in my mother's tallest boxwoods. She'd saved those boxwoods from some sort of rare fungus, and these boys were bouncing one another against their flexible skeletons.

I raised the hammer high above my head and charged toward the boys, yelling like a child playing Cowboys and Indians.

"He's got a hammer," someone yelled.

The boys broke through the bush and ran out the other side. I chased them all the way out of the yard. When I returned to the guesthouse, my friends fell silent and stared at me. I calmly replaced the hammer in the drawer and grabbed another handful of pretzels.

A girl announced that James Higgins was drunk and locked in his car, asleep. I'd considered doing the whole collection of car keys thing but quickly realized that a.) there were too many people, and b.) it would be easier to extract sex than car keys from some of these boys.

I walked to the driveway. Neil Hollis and David Ramer, two veritable charm machines, were sitting in the kitchen with our houseguest. She was in her nightgown, waving her hands and telling stories like an old movie star.

My mother peered out the window. "How's it going?" she asked.

"Never again," I said.

James was indeed passed out in the driver's seat. His keys were in the ignition and his interior light was on. I knocked on the window with my knuckles. When that failed to rouse him, I took a few pieces of gravel and tapped on the glass, making a sound like a housekeeper clicking her ring of keys against a hotel door. He came to and rolled down the window. I felt as if I was in one of those after-school specials in which well-groomed boys wrestle over a set of car keys.

I tried every conceivable line of persuasion. Finally he backed his car out of the driveway and sped off into the night.

I wandered back into the yard, feeling very Great Gatsby about the scene before me. Kids were slamming beers under the walnut tree, kissing by the fish pond, and throwing up in the garden. My limp attempt at civilizing this brood would go down in history as one of Lexington's least remarkable parties.

The party wound down organically. Many of my friends stayed and crashed on the floor. I didn't go to sleep that night, but watched the sun rise over a yard littered with the debris of adolescence. I wrote all night, since that was the only true escape from the swirl.

Before we picked up cans and bottles, I pushed play on the stereo to provide some accompaniment. The guitar-picked opening of "Sweet Home Alabama" wafted into the yard. My friends started dancing, swinging their trash bags from side to side. I let out a long, low groan. Then I started dancing, too.

pornography

The day after I got my driver's license, I took my mother's station wagon across the East Lexington bridge. It was close to midnight on a Tuesday, and I'd told my parents that I was going out for Diet Coke. My mother, who shared my habit, understood this late-night errand in a manner befitting a fellow addict.

I pulled into a gas station. After school earlier that day, I'd bought candy there, as well as a pack of cigarettes. I wasn't smoking, but I figured that the purchase would boost my believability as an eighteen-year-old when I tried to buy porn magazines later that evening. The man who owned the place was always there late and I'd calculated the shift changes over several visits. I'd heard they sold beer to minors, especially on his shifts, so I figured, even with my baby face, I could get away with buying smut.

I got out of the car and was careful to take money out of my wallet so that if he asked for proof of age, I could say I left my wallet at home. Teenagers plotting their illegalities are every bit as creative as politicians when it comes to inventing the truth. I still didn't have a fake ID, which would be worthless for me anyway. Everyone in town knew my family, and I always looked about four years younger than I was. Friends were using driver's licenses from older siblings or taking beer to the counter and just passing as older. I, on the other hand, had to work the phone, cultivating a network of older friends and acquaintances who would buy me beer and leave it on their back porch for me to retrieve.

I thought of my brother Hunter, who was an excellent role model because he taught me, above all, to remain calm while perpetrating. I closed my eyes and pushed on the door. Nothing. I turned the doorknob. Nothing. *Closed.* The sign read *Closed.*

Relieved but disappointed, I went back to the car and started the engine. Where could I get porn magazines at this hour? The truck stop? Definitely, but they're all behind the counter. Truck stops didn't carry gay porn, I knew, but I would have settled for anything. I could get a trucker to buy them for me. I'd done that with beer once. A trucker would understand the hormonal needs of a teenage boy better than anyone, since the profession involves so much masturbation. Some trucker would take pity on me and buy a titty magazine for me. The truckers would be there for me.

I turned onto Route 11. I started scheming about how maybe I could offer to buy dinner for the trucker to thank him. Maybe he'd take a liking to me. Maybe he'd call me *kiddo* and give me old magazines he'd been saving in his rig. Maybe he'd send me postcards from all over America. Maybe he'd take me up the coast on a long haul during my spring break.

The cop had to blast his siren at me twice, because the spinning blue lights failed to puncture my daydream. He pulled me over in the Kroger parking lot and asked me if I knew why he'd stopped me. I hate it when cops ask you that, especially when you know damn well why they stopped you. But I honestly didn't. I wasn't speeding, and my mother's Brady Wagon would *never* have a taillight missing.

"Because I was about to buy porn?" I thought. "Because I was having impure thoughts about a trucker buying me porn?"

"You don't have your headlights on," he said. The area was well lit and I'd left that gas station in a state of thrilled terror.

I was shaking visibly as I handed him my license and registration.

"You just got your license, boy."

"Yes, sir," I said.

The cop shined the flashlight right in my face, then handed my license and registration back to me.

"I'm not gonna write ya up, kid, but be careful. Tell your father that Buzz said howdy."

I thanked him profusely, and he walked back to the squad car, his flashlight beam bouncing along the road.

I pulled out onto the highway without turning my headlights on. A truck passed, flashing his lights at me. Finally, well on my way to the truck stop, I turned on my lights.

For my twelfth birthday, I had a slumber party. Mason Emore brought me the best birthday present I've ever received—a copy of Penthouse Letters *that he'd found in a trash can on the W&L campus. The pages were battered even before I got my hands on it. I read each story hundreds of times. The photos included the occasional man, but the text rarely included a guy unless it was one of the two "lesbian" stories which portrayed women having sex in a way that catered to straight male fantasy.*

One of the stories, "Air Force Lieutenant Takes Randy Hunk on a Fanciful Flight," told the story of two men who meet and blow each other during a fateful drunken evening. Part of the happy ending is that the narrator goes home to his girlfriend and vows never to do it again. He says he's glad he had the experience. I read that story over and over, careful not to ruin the pages with splashes of semen. That magazine was sacred to me. It was the reason I learned to restrict my orgasms, directing my gratification into my palm, so as not to destroy my bible.

Of course, I spent most of my fantasies imagining I was one of the women in the heterosexual stories, which were far hotter to me. No fumbling wannabe bi guys experimenting. The straight couples really went at it. In that long tradition of gay people losing them-

selves in opposite-sex characters, I was drawn to stories in which I could imagine myself beneath cowboys and postal workers. I trained my eyes to glaze over the occasional mention of phrases such as "her breasts."

Looking at magazine porn was a favorite slumber party activity. A friend had stolen several issues of Hustler *from his father, but I didn't care for them. There were no stories, only pictures, which ruined my ability to see myself in the magazines. Plainly put,* Hustler *had too many pink parts for an aspiring gay boy's brain to peacefully accommodate.*

You make do with whatever erotic materials you can get your hands on when you're a teenager. Sometimes it doesn't matter whether it's a man or a woman you're looking at. Sometimes just the fact that you're looking at something that is sexually explicit is enough to give your erotic imagination permission to wander. Teenagers deserve an infinite supply of permission. Everyone does.

I'd scoured the Richmond Yellow Pages for possibilities. Nothing under *Gay. Bookstores,* nope. *Adult Book Stores,* a few entries. *Novelties* was a euphemism for dildos, but one could never be sure that it wasn't a warehouse pushing juicemakers and disco hits compilations. Richmond always pops up as the address of those order-by-phone TV ads because it's full of such warehouses.

I'd carefully written out the name, address, and phone number of each listing in case I got lost. I didn't have the nerve to call beforehand and ask if they sold gay porn magazines, fearing that my voice would tip them off and ruin my chances when I actually showed up. I envisioned a bustling sales team behind the counter. As soon as I walked in, they'd whisper "That's the kid" and call the police. Thankfully, this was an instance in which my imagination truly was overactive.

The store was tiny. I parked out front after circling the block three times. I'd contemplated parking at the fast food place across the street, as I'm sure many patrons do, but imagined the manager would see me walk into the adult bookstore, write down my license plate, and have me towed. Everyone is out to get you when you're buying porn.

As I opened the door, a huge cowbell clunked twice. It was the most mortifying sound of my life up until that point. The three customers whipped around to look, and the sales clerk nodded at me. *Nodded* at me. Didn't throw me out. Didn't call the police. Nodded.

I scanned the room. There was an entire wall lined with rubber penises and devices I could neither afford nor comprehend. Still, I stood and took in the spectacle of it all—the blow-up dolls and fifteen-inch dildos, the black butt plugs and vibrating eggs. There were hundreds of items. It was at once overwhelming and comforting. I was both terrified and completely at home.

The entire place smelled of ammonia. I took a deep breath and learned to love that smell. To this day, when I smell ammonia, I think about courage.

I spotted the wall of gay porn magazines and slowly made my way across the room. I didn't want anyone to see how much I desperately wanted to gather up stacks of the magazines and run to my car. That's the game in an adult bookstore. People pretend they don't know what they're looking for. You don't see people making a beeline for the very thing they've been coveting for months. They make like they've just stumbled upon it by accident, like it's a rattlesnake.

All of the magazines were wrapped in cellophane, so I picked out several with men who held the most promise. I selected quickly, worried that I would be ejected for browsing. I cradled two magazines in front of me, the way teachers carry graded tests. I waited until the other customers left and slid the magazines onto the counter. The attendant was smoking a cigarette and watching *All My Children*. He barely looked at me as he rang up the sale. I handed him a twenty and chewed a hangnail. He wet his thumb to count off the ones into my hand.

As I turned to go, he looked at me over a pair of reading glasses and said, "Shouldn't do that."

I froze. I had the brown paper bag. I had my change. Surely he wasn't going to bust me *now.*

"Shouldn't bite your nails. Filthy habit." With that, he took a long drag off his cigarette and smiled at me.

I laid the brown bag on the passenger seat, nearly wrecking the car as I continually glanced at it as if to ensure that it still existed. I found a side street and parked the car, then tore open both magazines. The first, titled *Trade*, featured a construction worker on the cover. Inside, the models were very different from the guy on the cover—mostly street hustlers with bad teeth and very little body hair. They were young, dirty, and depraved-looking. One of the headings was "Street Chicken," which was the first time I'd ever encountered the word *chicken* in a sexual context. You could see little globs of white lube all over their hands, and some of their tattoos weren't finished. They were probably paid fifty bucks each.

When I looked at those pictures, I could feel a chorus of proverbial dirty old men staring at me. I felt as filthy as the young guys in the magazine. I closed the magazine and never looked at it again.

The second magazine was a collection of black-and-white stills from two 1970s porn movies. It was twelve dollars, printed on thick paper with high-quality photographs. The men were solid, bearded, and hairy. In the first set of pictures, a hiker happens upon a sunbather. The rest you can imagine. The second set of pictures was of a poolside sex scene and was so hot that it ruined me for every perfunctory pretty boy poolside romp that Falcon Studios has ever released. I'd glimpsed my future, and it was full of burly fortysomething men, bathed in the forgiving yellow light of seventies photography.

I jerked off in the car, keeping vigilant watch on the street and sidewalk. I carefully wiped up and returned the magazine, unsullied, to the brown paper bag.

I tried the next store on the list but it had closed. I found the third store, which looked like a converted garage. I walked in and started to browse the triple-wrapped bundles of back issue porn magazines. The man behind the counter asked me if I was eighteen. I said yes, and he asked to see my driver's license. I pretended to pat my pockets for my wallet, then told him I'd left it at home. He shrugged his shoulders and raised his eyebrows, which was the nicest way possible to kick me out.

When I was twenty-five, a friend loaned me a porn video called *Gold Rush Boys*. He promised it was my favorite sort of video, made in the 1970s with actors who were men, not bikini-waxed boys.

I popped it in the VCR. Thirty minutes later I hadn't hit fast forward even once, which says a lot in and of itself. I was transfixed. It was the movie that those stills had come from—the stills that nursed me through adolescence and midwifed hundreds of orgasms. Those photos were alive before me. What had once been thirty black-and-white photos was now sixty minutes of moving color pictures. I heard their voices, I saw their celebratory smiles, I saw their faces scrunch as they approached orgasm. These men who'd been the brothers, strangers, and daddies of my fantasies—they'd returned to me.

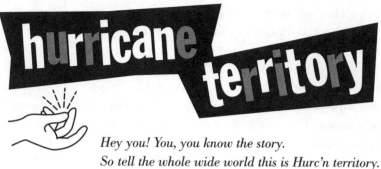

hurricane territory

Hey you! You, you know the story.
So tell the whole wide world this is Hurc'n territory.
—Lexington High School cheer

Football was the bane of my existence. Sophomore year, football season stretched on like the fucking Yellow Brick Road. We were winning, was the thing. We were winning a lot. For the first time in twenty-six years, Lexington High School made it to the state finals.

For those of you whose football teams never went to your state finals, let me break this down into manageable bite-sized pieces. We had months of pep rallies, everyone wore our school colors of red and white on a daily basis, and there were constant loud-speaker announcements wishing luck to Big Red. Even the Latin Club made a banner, in Latin, entreating the football team to "Kill!" If that doesn't bespeak excess, then I don't know what does.

Football games were a frightening spectacle to behold. Throngs of LHS students and drunk alumni huddled together on freezing bleacher seats, united by some deformed stepchild of nationalism. I couldn't even bear to cover my heart during the national anthem, let alone scream "It's hot out here! There must be a Hurc'n in the at-*mo*-sphere."

Cheerleaders, some of whom were my friends, jumped and kicked, screaming with voices that would someday corral children. I couldn't bear to walk by them during games, fearing that I'd smirk and reveal myself as a snide little prick.

I'd even considered going out for the football team. My brother urged me to walk on as their kicker, but I knew it wouldn't be that simple. I'd have to attend grueling daily practices, quit soccer, play third and fourth string at other positions, and subject myself to inevitable fag-baiting.

Part of it was a big ol' class thing. Many of those guys were hunters. They had pick-up trucks with gun racks. They were the same people who mumbled "faggot" as I passed them on the way to the cafeteria. I presumed that none of these boys were safe for me to be alone with in a hallway. Some proved me wrong.

One of the players, Bucky Hilton, had a gay brother. It was never discussed, and his brother didn't come out until years later, but it was pretty obvious. When there's a sissy in a country family, it's like hearing a flute in the middle of a string quartet.

When we were twelve, Freddy and I bonded over monster trucks, cigars, and heavy metal. We'd camp out in the backyard and build bonfires that usually attracted the police. On top of the hill overlooking his house, we learned how to smoke cigars together. We'd even reached the point where it was okay to be nauseous in front of each other. He wanted to try dipping tobacco, but I couldn't even bring myself to touch the crap with my fingers, let alone stuff it under my lip.

Freddy taught me the characters and dilemmas necessary to follow the soap opera that is pro wrestling. I introduced him to the Sex Pistols. It was an even swap.

I still see Freddy when I go home for Christmas. He'll be sitting at the local bar with all the other LHS graduates who have resorted to draft beer to avoid their families. Sometimes we'll talk, sometimes we'll just nod at one another. After his brother came out, Freddy told Johnna that he respects me. I told Johnna I thought he'd grown cuter with age. But I don't think she relayed that one to Freddy.

Of course, one must never downplay the cute factor when discussing high school football. As much as the sport repulsed me, some of the guys were adorable. The coaches were even cuter and satisfied my insatiable appetite for intellectually inferior authority figures. The coaches made pep rallies bearable because they *dressed up*. For a *pep rally*. Otherwise, I'd have skipped. The coaches would come in with their freshly polished cowboy boots and neckties. They'd put goo in their hair and feather comb it into about four hundred layers. I didn't know whether to try to jump their bones or buy an insurance policy from them. The pep rallies were chore-ographed hormonal exchanges between the football players and cheerleaders. The spit-shined coaches would preen like elder tribesmen. I always sat on the front row, adapting a bit of Mrs. Tucci's advice: *You'll hate it, but at least you can write about it.*

The night before the team went to Lunenberg, wherever *that* was, to play in the state finals, we had a huge bonfire behind the school. People were getting crazy, dancing around the fire and screaming. It was like some sort of tent revival. I hung back and wrote in my journal. Retreat was the only safe option, what with the demonic mob mentality. The Scarlet Hurricanes were rais-ing the dead with that bonfire. I could see spirits wafting above the burning cardboard boxes. It was like a scene from *The Crucible*. Could anyone see those ghosts? They'd summoned up the ancestry, and for what? *Football.*

The night the team returned from their victory, everyone in town went to the high school to meet the buses. People were crying and shit. They hoisted hand-lettered signs above their heads, proclaiming things like "Congradulatiens Big Red!" These boys were their children and friends' children. People held aloft babies in red-and-white outfits, as if for sacrifice. Everyone was blowing whistles and honking those obnoxious airhorns and throwing confetti. And they'd dressed up. Either they were in red-and-white outfits or their church clothes.

I walked through the crowd, studying their faces. A sixty-year-old man wore an old LHS letter jacket. He stood next to his son, also in a letter jacket. Both bobbed up and down, trying to catch a glimpse of the boys stepping off the buses in their jerseys. They would be wearing those jerseys around town for years to come.

"There he is," the younger man screamed. "There he is!" He pointed at his own son, who was stepping off the bus. The father shook his fist, hooting. The older man was crying. Then they both were. They held onto each other and jumped up and down together. Their voices broke and rattled, but they kept yowling.

These were my people, like it or not. These were the friends and neighbors I'd been given. Someday maybe they would love me as they loved the boys stepping off that bus. Maybe, if I worked at it, if I let myself be one of them, if I established my place.

When I go home to Lexington, I always visit my teachers at the high school. I always walk through town, saying hello to people in the community. Every year, I check in with the town pharmacists, the librarians, the ministers, and the bank tellers. They all know I'm gay. Many of them held me when I was a baby. It's important to me that they watch me grow up, that they trace my development from child to teenager to young adult, and eventually, middle age. If you can look someone in the eye and say, "I knew you when you were *this* big," it's hard to hate them. Gay men and women cannot just disappear from our hometowns. That's where we have the most influence.

I never wanted to abandon Lexington altogether. I never wanted to be one of those people who doesn't return for their high school reunions. In my heart of hearts, I loved Lexington and LHS. I loved the people I'd grown up with and even when they scared me, I held out hope that they'd come around on gay issues.

It always infuriates me when I hear people dismiss poor Southerners as ignorant bigots. Some of the folks who've loved me the hardest have been country people, trailer people, farm people. It can be a challenge to go home and explain to them what

I'm doing with my life, because their realities are so entirely different from mine. My exposure to sexual adventure, college, and radical politics has created painful cultural differences between us. But they're my people, and I can't give up on them.

I stepped to the edge of the sidewalk and started screaming along with the crowd. During all those months of pep rallies, it was the first time I'd thrown my voice into the mix. The football players were running around the parking lot, slapping hands, kissing their mothers and whatnot. The cheerleaders were tossing white plastic footballs into the crowd. It was the first time I remember giving a shit about the Hurricanes.

"Go Big Red!" I screamed, then stopped, realizing that they'd already *gone* and that after winning at state, they didn't need to *go* anymore.

"Good job, Red!" I yelled. My school spirit needed rehearsals.

One of the plastic footballs popped me on the head, then bounced into the street, where a group of five grown women wrestled for it. The woman who emerged with the ball tucked it under her vintage LHS sweatshirt to safeguard it from snatchers. Her hair was a standard-issue cheerleader do: overpermed, sides sprayed into curly wings, puffed bangs towering four inches above her forehead.

"I used to be the one throwin' these," she said. "If it hits you on the head, you get to keep it."

"Is that how you picked your husband?" I asked her, sounding a lot like the Colonel.

"I reckon so," she laughed, then handed me the football.

One of the after-parties was thrown by my niece. A party of this magnitude could only mean one thing—my brother and his wife were out of town.

I could hear Jimmy Buffett from half a mile away. The victory kept neighbors from phoning the cops about the party. Drunk football players and their admirers littered the lawn. I parked as close as I could, two houses away, and turned off my car. I restarted the car and listened to the Smiths' "Shoplifters of the World Unite and Take Over." It would be my last dose of such music for hours.

By the time I reached the house, the music had shifted to Hank Williams Jr.'s "A Country Boy Can Survive." Can you say culture shock? I was walking into it.

It was an outside party, which meant that my niece had the sense not to let those folks inside to trash the house. On the patio, a handful of Lexington High School's finest were sucking down beers and puffing amateurishly on cigarettes. As guests arrived, everyone screamed out the newcomer's name.

It was freezing out. High school kids go to great lengths to drink flat keg beer. Sitting outside on cold patio furniture or, worse, cold bricks, did not strike me as the stuff of revelry. Some of the guys were so drunk on beer and high on adrenaline that they'd stripped down to tee shirts as they tossed a football in the driveway. A drunk football player motioned to me that he was going to toss me a spiral. I politely declined. It's all fun and games until the gay boy drops it.

I went inside the house to find my niece and several others sitting on the couch.

"Kirkus!" she shrieked, getting up to hug me.

"Hey kids," I replied. I looked around my brother's living room. "Haven't been *here* in a while." The room grew silent. I was *such* a buzz kill.

I wandered out into the garage and struck up a conversation with my nephew Carlton, who is a year my junior. All of this chaos was swirling around us and there he sat, strumming his guitar. He tried to engage me in a discussion of Bob Dylan's mid-career lyrics. I wasn't smoking pot in those days, which probably would have made me less acerbic. He offered to play me a song he'd just written. I think it was about smoking pot and being less acerbic.

When he finished, I said, "I can't go out there. Those people don't understand me. I hate those idiots."

Carlton looked at me with his big soulful been-through-it-all eyes and said, "Then stay inside."

He played and we sang together. We'd played at a café together several times. My singing left much to be desired, but we made up for this by covering songs in which I could do character voices, like the Black Crowes' "She Talks to Angels" and Jane's Addiction's "Jane Says." Just being around him calmed me down.

He'd recently grown out his nappy hair, taken up painting, and reinvented himself as a hippie. Carlton went from a math/science jock to an Earth-loving peacenik in a matter of months. He seemed to get along with the people I wanted to strangle.

One of the football players staggered into the garage. He knocked over a chair and tripped on the carpet. I was ready to have him arrested, but Carlton just patted the space on the sofa beside him and said, "Hey Jimmy, why don't you come have a seat."

Jimmy was enormous. He lumbered over, a cigarette smoldering between his teeth. No one was supposed to smoke in the house, but Carlton calmly handed him an empty beer can for ashes. Then he started playing "Teach Your Children." We both sang. It was totally cheesy.

During the chorus, Jimmy joined in with *"And know they love you."*

I'd have puked from the sentiment except that it all felt so genuine.

Jimmy got up as the song ended, said "Thank you, boys," and dragged himself out onto the patio.

"You're a snake charmer," I told Carlton.

"I just talk to people," he said. "Like Grandaddy does."

He played several Eagles songs, which brought people into the garage for a drunken sing-along. Once there were ten people in the room, I nodded to Carlton and walked out. He'd worked his magic.

I said good night to my niece and headed toward the rear door of the garage. Jimmy grabbed my arm and pulled me through the doorway and into a patio chair. I tensed up, thinking maybe he was going to hit me. Sloppily, he sat down next to me and slapped me on the back.

"Hey," he said. "You know, I heard what people say about you. I don't know if it's true or not and I don't really care. You know what? I think you're one hell of a guy."

With that, Jimmy slapped me on the back again and handed me a pizza box.

"I want you to have this," he said. "You're one hell of a guy."

I opened the box. There were three pieces of cold cheese pizza and a pile of crusts.

"Wow," I said. "Thanks."

"You're welcome."

"Um, why don't you have a piece? Here."

I handed him a piece of the pizza and took one for myself. We sat on the patio, in silence, eating our slices. I held the box in my lap as if it was an Oscar.

He inhaled that piece and I handed him the third. "Here. You should keep your strength up."

"I hear you got a big kick," he said. "Soccer, huh?"

"Yeah. Um, thanks," I stammered. "Good job today. That's awesome that you won," I said. I couldn't believe that those words had crossed my lips.

"Thanks, man."

"Sure."

That night, I cut the lid off that pizza box and added it to my ceiling collage of pizza boxes. Yes, I had such a thing. I also had an entire wall of Wrigley gum wrappers, a wall of obituaries, and a wall of Diet Coke labels. Mom disliked the pizza box lids more than anything because of the grease spots which she said would attract bugs. I taped the one Jimmy gave me away from the others, so that it was right over my pillow. I'd received benediction, and there would be mornings when I needed to be reminded of that.

audience

Dancing in the mirror
and you're on the other side.
—The Ninth

There was always an audience on the other side of the mirror—a huge, roaring rock concert audience.

Some nights I played guitar, scissor-kicking and throwing my arms in Pete Townsend windmills. Some nights I was the cool, detached bass player, nodding my head and cutting my eyes like Kim Gordon of Sonic Youth. Some nights I pulled up the armchair and played ferocious drums, making dumb drummer faces at the crowd and playing more rolls than the song required. But most nights I was Michael Stipe.

The first time I saw R.E.M. was in Fairfax on their Work tour, right after they released *Document*. It was the last college radio album they ever made. Rich took me. I gave our third ticket to my neighbor Sammy, my adopted little brother. I'd decided it was my responsibility to feed him good music, bring him concert tee shirts, and teach him about life's most important pastimes: smoking and masturbating. As we walked through the parking lot, I heard some college brat blurt "Hey, that kid in the Meat Puppets shirt is like *twelve*." And yes, actually, he was.

I already loved R.E.M., but I wasn't yet a fan. 10,000 Maniacs opened for them before anyone knew who Natalie Merchant was. She did her whole spin-dancing peasant-girl thing. It was fabulous. This was before the Versace, before she started making socially conscious videos.

That night, R.E.M. played beneath a shimmering screen full of arty projections. Fish swam, Stipe wore black eye makeup. Windmills spun, Stipe twirled. That man cast a spell so vivid and holy that I was ready to hide in the truck that held the amps. After seeing this, how could I return to high school?

I'd seen plenty of concerts by that point. My most embarrassing concert was Mötley Crüe and Whitesnake at the Roanoke Civic Center. My mother dropped two friends and me off at 1 P. M. so we could wait in line with all the other gawky metalheads.

Andrea Vaughn and Kerri Lynn had picked their favorite band members. Andrea liked Nikki Sixx and Kerri liked Tommy Lee. They were always careful not to like the same guy. Bon Jovi was their band of choice, though. They'd written the names of Richie Sambora and Jon Bon Jovi in black Magik Marker on their clothes in preparation for that concert. Since they weren't technically *in love* with the guys from Mötley Crüe, they were considerably low-key. The three of us sat in line for six hours, smoking cigarettes and trying to look as bad-ass as possible to impress the other headbangers. I had a Metallica patch on my jean jacket and wore a Skinny Puppy tee shirt. I wanted people to know that I was a punk with metal leanings. I was not merely a Ratt or Poison fan, for God's sake. I had standards. I was thirteen.

The second time I saw R.E.M., Rich scored stageside seats for Shelley and me, which were better than floor seats because there was no one in front of us. Drivin' n' Cryin' opened and proved to be much harder-edged than we'd expected. I bought something like six tee shirts before the show even started, then regretted it because I didn't want to have to watch them all night. The lights went out.

Shelley and I started jumping up and down, squealing like kids at a McDonald's playcenter. We grabbed the railing in front of us. Footage from their home video *Succumbs* splattered the screen. Stipe came out in a long black coat and the band launched into "Pop Song '89." The screen flashed words from the lyrics: *HELLO, GOVERNMENT, WEATHER*. After each song, Stipe took off another layer of clothing until he was shirtless. His long braided ponytail hung down his back. I asked Shelley how long it took hair to grow, since she had really long hair. She said a half-inch per month, and that's if you're really lucky. I'd never make it.

Rich and I had gathered some bootleg live shows from the Fables and Pageantry tours, so we knew Stipe's *a capella* moments by heart. We sang so loud that Peter Buck looked at us. Mike Mills even waved. God, we must have looked ridiculous. Before the opening strains of "Finest Worksong," Stipe growled *"Dig . . . this."* He sang through a megaphone. He did this freaky little dance where he shuffled his feet, popped his arm out and wiggled his shoulders. I couldn't wait to get home in front of the mirror so I could try it.

My favorite song, "World Leader Pretend," involved Stipe beating a chair with a drumstick. I watched slackjawed. On the way home, I lay in the backseat of Rich's car and wrote down every song in order. I wrote down every word of Stipe's between-song patter. I wrote down every projection, every outfit, every gesture, every altered lyric. I ended up missing school so I could see the next few shows in North Carolina. Later in the tour, I caught one of their final shows in Roanoke. It's a damn good thing I was never given to stalking. Reverent study was quite enough, thank you.

The full-length mirror in my room was right next to the stereo. I played DJ for myself, picking songs from around a thousand cassettes and five hundred records. I'd dubbed hundreds of albums from friends and padded my collection by repeatedly sending in fake names to record clubs. When I received the twelve free albums or tapes, I'd write the company a letter saying no one by that name lived at this address. Legally, the company couldn't require me to return merchandise that was wrongfully sent. Of course, legally, I was racking up one hell of a lot of fraud charges. But I got an amazing record collection out of it.

As I started my performances, I opened the closet and dressed as much like a rock star as my wardrobe allowed. I dressed in layers like Stipe and threw off clothes during my concert. I lip-synched. Sometimes, if my parents weren't home, I'd really sing.

I wore sunglasses, then tossed them onto the bed. I wore hats and scarves. I wore boots. I went barefoot. I wore bracelets and rings. I put socks over my hands. I pulled my hair back with a bandana. I wore big coats. I wore ties. I wore hand-lettered tee shirts. I wore nothing.

In that mirror, I was a rock star. I could hear the screams between songs and I could see lighters burning during power ballads. I moved all the furniture so I could make my entrance, walking the length of the room until I grabbed the microphone. I shook the mike stand and stalked around the stage, pumping my fist as big guitar parts came in. I jumped on the foot locker, stomping out the bass drum parts. I slithered across the carpet. I danced and sang until I was drenched in sweat. When it was late, I wore headphones and never explained to my parents why I took so many showers in the middle of the night. It's a teenage thing, they must have thought.

I was Patti Smith and I was Ace Frehley. I was Darby Crash and I was Billy Bragg. I was Bob Marley and James Hetfield and Joe Strummer and Sid Vicious. I was Jello Biafra and Bob Mould and all four Ramones. But most nights I was Michael Stipe. While the rest of the world was asleep, I was Michael Stipe.

fullbacks

You know how soccer teams on television flit their lithe European bodies up and down the length of the field making fifty passes per minute? The Rockbridge Rebels were not like that. We were every inch the rogue hick-town team, more likely to elbow the other team's captain in the belly than to trap a fly ball between our thighs. Actually, we weren't even a school team, we were a club team. Lexington High School wouldn't officially recognize soccer or lacrosse, the sports of choice for "preps" or, as some county kids referred to us, the "R&F"—the Rich and Famous.

We weren't overly skilled and knew we were in trouble when we played snooty private schools like Virginia Episcopal and Woodberry Forest. They'd do their Pelé passes and run three times as fast as any of us. Many of us smoked cigarettes and got high after practice, so we weren't models of fitness. We didn't even wear matching socks. Plus, the referees at private schools were far less tolerant of our sole defensive strategy: pushing.

Our coaches were three W&L students, one of whom I had, you guessed it, developed a crush on. I never gave him any of the poems I wrote to him, which were filled with references to his icy blue eyes and gooey autumnal imagery. Self-respect dictates that one may write only so many such poems in a single lifetime. I'd about hit that quota.

Twice a year we played Shenandoah Christian, which always meant that we'd act satanic and pull out our best Jesus jokes.

Jarred affected a mock crucifixion pose seconds before kickoff, then said to our opponents, "Don't leave me hangin', bro!"

We peppered our on-field speech with exclamations of "Jesus Christ!" and "Goddamn!" It mostly rattled their cheerleaders, who'd respond with peppy, faith-based chants. The team actually prayed during their huddle, whereas we were more likely to select which opponents we wanted to maim.

Valerie had been demoted to mascot. Whenever we played a Christian school, they'd bring their damn cheerleaders on a bus— to a *soccer* game, mind you. Our games drew, at most, sixteen people. What troops were these Christians rallying? The Christian schools wouldn't let our girls play, which infuriated Valerie. It was delicious to watch her razz God's pep squad, because she had, until recently, been such a devout Holy Roller herself. I could see her from the field, wagging her finger at the cheerleaders, lecturing them about subservience. Then again, the girls were all wearing miniskirts, so maybe Valerie was less politically driven than I imagined at the time.

Today's game was emotional for us. The last time we'd played these Christian soldiers, one of them kicked our goalie Kent in the face so hard he'd lost depth perception in his left eye. He and I grew up down the street from each other, and he was in many ways my brother.

So the grudge was especially bloody. In our pre-game huddle, we all noted the guy's number and where he was playing. He was a forward. I was a fullback. He turned out to be my man.

I wasn't terribly intent on winning the game, just on taking that guy out. Every time he flew down the field with the ball, I'd sidle up to him and drive my cleat into one of his knees. I wanted him in the hospital, where he'd put Kent. He knew I was roughing him, and when it was just the two of us in the corner or along the sideline, he'd whine things like "Leave me alone, man" or

"Get *off* me." It sent spectators into fits of giggles and gave me further encouragement to slide tackle him.

My coaches could see what I was doing, and they told me to ease up and follow the ball. I wanted one last chance. Our new goalie tossed the ball to me and I delayed clearing it up the line. It bounced twice, and suddenly, there was Jesus Boy, all over me. As soon as he stepped in front of me, I threw my leg out and "missed" the ball, dragging my cleats across his thigh. I'd scraped away a fair amount of skin and it was enough to make him curl up on the ground. There was a little blood, but not nearly enough. Not enough to take him out.

At this point, the Colonel was pacing the length of the field, shouting obnoxious paternal aphorisms like "Don't get mad, get even." Dad had retired, which meant he was even busier, showing up for half a game or less, then disappearing to some community organization meeting. Dad hated when I played rough or cussed. "Be noble," he'd urge. "*Be gracious.*"

I got a yellow card for that one. The referee rushed up and wrote down my number on a notepad. I acted defiant as he made silly referee gestures, yelled "Charge!" and gave the other team a direct kick against us. As they lined up the ball, I wondered how I was going to hurt this guy seriously without getting kicked off the team.

Kent, on the other hand, possessed old-school sportsmanship. He didn't go for blood. He played hard and would clash when necessary, but he just played the ball. Such peaceful tactics eluded me altogether.

Near the end of the second half, we needed a goal to tie us up. The game had escalated into a series of elbow digs and overt shoves. Each team was regularly taking a direct kick from various crime scenes. Near the middle of the field, Kent lined up the kick.

"Let Kirk take it," my coach called out. "Kirk, you take it."

Determined to make me a jock, my brother Hunter had coached my kicking incessantly. He stood ten feet in front of me and had me chip the ball into his hands hundreds of times in a row. He drove me to football fields and taught me how to kick thirty-yard field goals. He fashioned kicking tees from molded balls of aluminum foil. He videotaped failed field goal attempts by NFL stars and had me watch them repeatedly. Even when it rained, Hunter would continue rolling the ball to me. Mud splattered all over us. His hands stung as the wet leather landed in his palms.

"Get your knee over it, look straight ahead, then lean back. Let it fly," he'd shout, all coachy. "You can make a thirty-yard kick."

"Yeah, but there aren't twenty guys charging at me," I'd reply.

Undaunted, he gave me football cards featuring field goal kickers. His favorite team was the Redskins; naturally, his fantasy was that I would be the next Mark Moseley.

"Moseley's gonna retire soon," he'd say, encouraging me to join the football team. Hunter could memorize the statistics on the card's flip side in a matter of seconds. I thought Mark was cute, so the picture was the extent of my interest. It was about as close as we ever came to agreement in the matter of football, but it left me with a big kick.

"Boot it, Kirk!" Connie Flint screamed from the sidelines in a raspy Rockbridge County drawl. We'd played soccer together for years, until her track coach forced her to quit.

"Knock the shit outta that ball!" Connie also had a mouth on her.

I lined up the ball. Jesus Boy stepped in front of me, as close as he could get.

"You want some?" I said, glaring at him. It was one of those icky bravado moments you see in high school football movies.

Jesus Boy stepped aside, knowing I'd try to sterilize him if he didn't.

I knew I couldn't drop it right in front of one of our forwards. That was a Euro move. So I kicked it as hard as I could. As my foot made contact, I looked directly at Jesus Boy, then leaned back. I nailed it. The ball went soaring above his head.

The ball sank from the sky, heading toward the goal. I charged at Jesus Boy, looking for another excuse to kick him. The ball dropped into the top right corner, so high the goalie barely tried to make the save.

My junior year, I volunteered to coach a Little League soccer team. I'd watched various coaches carefully during my ten years of play. I saw the star system develop each time autumn rolled around. Some kids played half a game while others played all four quarters. Girls always played half a game. The little uncoordinated kids always played half a game. And everyone, from the very first day of practice, seem to know their assigned positions already.

Youth soccer had a kind of caste system in which fast kids played forward and scored goals, fat kids were assigned to fullback—the left field of soccer—where they'd do the least amount of damage, and the hyperactive kids who hadn't been dosed with Ritalin made natural midfielders and were expected to follow the ball wherever it went. No one, of course, wanted to play goalie.

My assistant coach was a man three times my age whose son was on the team. The team included two sets of brothers and a few cousins. This made it easier for parents to pick up children and it made for continuous family drama.

When I was five, my first team had been the Bobcats. We had light salmon-colored jerseys and I was a fullback. I was a bit chubby. I didn't actually play that much soccer, because I was madly in love with Shelley Jansen, also a chubby fullback. During games, we'd stand in front of the goal holding hands or picking our noses. During a particularly heavy match, our coach, a burly bearded man, intervened. He ran onto the field, picked me up, and ran with me to the center of the field, then plopped me down.

"When the ball goes down the field, you go with it!" he screamed.

Laughter erupted from the sidelines, and I stood at midfield while the opposing team burned past me to score one of many goals that day. Shelley and I couldn't be bothered with such mortal pursuits, and we relished the quarters in which we warmed the bench together, gorging ourselves on orange slices.

I played fullback exclusively for several years until an Italian coach decided that I was the team's "big kick" and that I should play forward. Dad always insisted that I'd inherited my mother's logo, a compliment that never seemed to please her much. The coach let me be part of that season's star system and I scored my first goals that season. The Colonel was dizzy with pride and started snapping pictures obsessively at games.

Predictably, I nursed a ferocious crush on this coach. He often mixed up verbs, screaming *juggle* instead of *dribble* and *post* instead of *pass*. His lapses in language made him all the more irresistible to a certain lovesick ten-year-old.

My brief season as a star reminded me how much fun soccer was supposed to be. The kids on the team I coached were between nine and eleven years old, so they'd only been playing for three or four years. Still, each came to practice with a position branded on his or her forehead. Some coach had decided where they would play for the next ten years. How much fun could that be?

Only one kid had never played before. The child of hippie parents, he'd been home-schooled and wasn't accustomed to being around other kids. He left several practices in tears. As he climbed into his family's station wagon, the rest of the team huddled. Several of the boys tossed out words such as *sissy* and *wuss*, and I made the entire team run eight laps as punishment. It was my sole drill sergeant moment. After that, it was really clear that such insults would not be tolerated.

Many of the other coaches I played under never had a game plan or even a roster. So, at the end of the game, they'd realize that some of us had only played two quarters. Parents pitched the occasional fit. My parents were of the coaches-and-teachers-are-always-right school, so they were never among the stampede of pissy guardians. Invariably, the kids who saw little play disappeared under the bleachers, where they'd goof off, cry, or find trouble with other forgotten children. I wasn't interested in perpetuating this.

I drew meticulous grids for games to ensure that each child played at least three quarters. The kids who played four quarters were rotated from game to game. Players were shuffled around the field so that they played several positions during each game. One of the star players gave me lip when he realized he wasn't scoring as much as usual, but I was stubborn as hell.

From the sidelines, I screamed and coaxed. I found the bass in my voice and channeled some serious coach energy. This was no small task. I've never been one of those sports fans who yells at referees and calls for the blood of the opposition. But these were my kids, and their tiny limbs brought out a primal protective instinct in me. I pulled them out when they mouthed off at a ref. I worried like a mother when they didn't wear long underwear beneath their jerseys. I held their jewelry and watches for them. Regardless of how few goals we scored, we always had the most creative 2-4-6-8 chants. A flood of gratitude overwhelmed me every time one of them called me Coach.

They asked me repeatedly if I had a girlfriend. I always said no, but if I'd had a boyfriend, I would have said so. I was already the youngest coach the league had ever seen, so I was feeling enough pressure to keep parents happy. I didn't want to deal with the possible ramifications. To my surprise, the parents liked me despite our losing streak. It's always more fun to win, but I knew from experience that winning teams usually leave one-third of their members disappointed.

The following spring, I came out in an article in the local newspaper. I'd written a gay-themed play that was going to be produced in Richmond. Several of the kids I coached came to see it. They were eleven and twelve years old by then. I can only imagine what sorts of conversations they had with their parents. In the lobby of the theater, two of them ran toward me. They'd seen the play, they knew I was a big fag.

"Good job, Coach," they said, slapping my hands.

They're out of college now, which makes me feel ancient. When I see those kids today, they still call me Coach. It still makes me tingle.

cute

"Kirk 'Stud Man' Read," the camp counselor announced, prompting screams and whistles from 250 people. It was mail call, which, defying all conventional reason, was handled piece by piece. After lunch, every attendee of the Table Rock Arts Camp gathered in the auditorium for this daily ritual. Every letter and package was announced, and the campers filed up to the stage to retrieve their loot.

As soon as I sat down with my letter, I was called up again.

"Kirk 'Honey Lips' Read," he said, holding a package aloft.

This went on each day for what seemed like hours. I'd receive approximately a dozen pieces of mail, addressed with completely mortifying monikers.

The summer between tenth and eleventh grades, my parents signed me up for the two-week arts camp, nestled in North Carolina's Smoky Mountains. The day they dropped me off, I was swarmed by girls. I thought it was a big joke at first, some sort of mix-up in the romantic food chain. By the third day of mail call, however, I realized that this brief period of perceived allure would haunt me for two solid weeks.

Girls did my laundry. They chased me all the way to the doorway of the boys-only dorm. They carried my tray in the cafeteria and fought over who would sit next to me. They screamed when I passed them. *Screamed.* I wish I was making this up, I really do. It was terrifying.

In sixteen years, I'd never been called cute before. This was a coveted term reserved for bona fide studs like Brandon Forester. All the time I'd played therapist and mascot for heartsick girls, I'd taken myself out of the running for cute status.

Meanwhile, the poetry instructor I was busily courting with bad all-lowercase poems found the entire situation amusing.

"God has an amazing sense of humor," he said.

I wrote him a feverish letter asking for advice on how to handle these attentions and he wrote back, "Don't worry about the little girls. Someday you'll find yourself a woman."

What in the hell would I do with a *woman?*

It was the age-old tale of teenage girls spewing and fluttering over a budding gay boy. He's sensitive, they marvel. He listens to me, they gush. He's polite and respectful and well-dressed and sweet and creative and *my parents would love him.* So, employing various strategies, these girls went about making me their own personal boyfriend.

My roommate was a long-haired muscleman who'd hooked up with the prettiest blonde at camp the very night he arrived. When girls serenaded me from beneath our window, he egged them on.

"Enjoy the chicks, man," he said in flawless straight-boy vernacular. He was incredulous that I hadn't had sex with any of them. I wanted to go *home.*

By the second week, I felt stalked, like Ringo in *A Hard Day's Night.* Finally, the five girls to whom I was closest accepted that I was looking only for friends. They slowed their pursuit and even stopped mailing the embarrassing parcels. Eventually, most of them found other boyfriends and allowed me to fall into the comfortable role of confidante. But by that point, it was too late. So many girls had started sending me letters and packages that it was no longer within the control of my original five admirers. Toward the end of camp, girls were sending me panties, whipped cream, and dog collars. It was amazing what one could find in the local grocery store. The nicknames they wrote on the outside of packages became so X-rated that counselors were announcing my name as "Kirk 'Bleep' Read."

To avoid them, I holed up in the boys' dorm with a small group of cigarette-smoking boys, all of whom played guitar. They taught me how to play R.E.M. songs, how to harmonize, and how to act aloof so that "skanky girls" lost interest.

"I want them *all* to lose interest," I said.

"Gotta save at least one or two," one advised. "Spare pussy comes in handy, man."

That summer was a straight boy's wet dream, having girls descend like locusts. But I'd made up my mind. It was a far better thing to be a member of the slumber party where cute boys are discussed.

I told my parents this harrowing tale on the five-hour drive home. I even showed them some of my spoils—the cake icing, the giant metal corkscrew, the chocolate syrup. I withheld the graphic missives. But they got the point.

The Colonel was half-thrilled and half-disturbed. Later the evening we got back, he pulled his car around to the front of the house and said, "Get in."

Once we reached the county line, he began ranting about women. Mom was his fourth wife, so whatever bitterness Dad harbored against women was being passed to his youngest son disguised as wisdom. He began explaining where babies come from, linking it to the manipulative schemes of women. They'd try to get me into bed, he told me, so that they could *control* me.

"Dad, I'm sixteen, I know this already."

"Keep your pecker in your pants," he said, shaking his finger. And that was the extent of our father-son talk.

When I compared notes with my siblings years later, it turns out that we all got variations on that same cautionary diatribe. Dad told my sisters that men would try to get them into bed so that they could get them pregnant—so they could *control* them. Parents are most loveable when you find out how faithfully they repeat themselves.

The next afternoon, my mother sat down in the den with me. She said she wanted to talk to me about something important. I thought someone had died.

"You're growing up," she said, "and I know you don't know which way you're swinging."

I froze. This was worse than the day the Colonel taught me to shave.

"I've known for a long time," she said. I didn't say anything because I just wanted her to stop talking. Each word felt like a punch to the gut. "You're more sensitive than my other kids. I worry about your heart."

"Mom . . . ," I groaned. It was like I'd been caught stealing—stealing panties.

"I love you," she said.

I couldn't look at her, I was too rattled by this reverse confession.

"Okay," she said, "that's all I wanted to say." She stood up and, for some reason, slammed the door hard behind her.

My mother had just done my coming-out for me.

river

In July, a woman from the Fine Arts Department of Rockbridge County called to ask if I'd be Willy Wonka in their summer musical.

The dirty little secret of children's theater is that if you're an adult or older teenager, you're automatically a babysitter. Between songs, I bounced five-year-olds on my lap and played patty-cake with prepubescent girls who whispered in my ear that they *liked* me. I could certainly empathize, because our director, Jim, was a stocky, older mountain man with sandy hair and a sly grin. And I *liked* him.

Sandra Carrer choreographed our dance routines. To my chagrin, the little kids picked up the twirls and box steps a lot faster than I did. Plus, I had to do all that crap with a top hat and a cane. My exposure to dance had been purely as a spectator. My friends Johnna and Kate were constantly having dance recitals. Preston Watts and I both threatened our parents with plans to take dance lessons. We would do it in solidarity, and we'd make sure we were given more to do than lift girls. Neither of us went through with it.

I had one solo in the show, a maudlin number titled "Life, What Is It But a Dream?" There was a lyrical reference to a stream, which presumably referred to the chocolate river in the play. That was the sum total of the song's relevance. I had to be heav-

---

how i learned to snap

ily coached by the musical director, to enunciate *"every word!"* and to avoid "chicken neck," a curious condition in which a singer bobs his neck back and forth as he sings. One of Jim's many directorial notes to me was that my singing was "scaring the children."

By the time we got to technical rehearsals, I was decked out in all of our local thrift shops' finery, plus enough black eyeliner to make me resemble a quarterback on a sunny Saturday morning. I missed our most important tech rehearsal when friends got me seventeenth-row seats to see the Who in Charlotte, but Jim, a former hippie, seemed to understand. "Don't scream at the concert," he said. I screamed at the concert.

Opening night went well enough. The thing about children's theater is that the audience is so fixated on their own kids, whether they're onstage or not, that everyone else is totally immaterial. After the Saturday matinée, Jim told me I was so flat that his toenails still hadn't uncurled. I was crushed, because I'd been scrawling obsessive journal entries about his every word and deed. I'd even written a poem about the production. It was not a thinly veiled declaration of love this time, but the gesture of handing it to him was, and emphatically so.

The next day, after the last performance, Jim spared me a final evaluation. As I was cold creaming and scrubbing copious amounts of gel out of my hair, he asked me to be an apprentice at a retreat for playwrights. He'd shown my poem to the director of the retreat, and they wanted me to be in the company. It involved some acting, lots of grunt work, and full immersion in the production of new scripts. What he didn't mention, of course, was that I would get to see him on a daily basis, which was the most compelling reason I was coming up with. I left that out when I lobbied my parents that evening.

Dad thought the company was a cult and that I would be exploited for free labor. I glared at him.

"Theater *is* a cult, Colonel," I said. "Just like the army."

He and Mom pow-wowed, then she sat me down in the den.

"You're going to be around a lot of people who have sex and use drugs," she said.

God, I hoped that was true.

"You're very vulnerable," she said.

"It's a great opportunity, Mom."

"I don't want your heart to break," she said.

Was she reading my journal? She had to be.

"I don't think you should go. You're still so undecided. I worry about that."

"I have to go," I said.

And I did go. I got in my little blue car and drove forty-five minutes north to the retreat, just outside Staunton.

When I arrived, I was hit full-on with the realization that I was *not* a theater person. Everyone there was a theater person. They were all on the deck of a huge barn, stretching, vocalizing, and smoking cigarettes. I did none of these things on a regular basis. I sat down in the corner and commenced filling my journal with more angsty mush.

A bearded man with wild eyes and rainbow suspenders gathered everyone in a circle, then told us we were going to do an exercise exploring our "communal energy." I'd done my sixth-grade term paper on the correlation between the Beatles' *White Album* and the Manson murders. This man was a dead ringer for Charlie, and he had the whole charisma-thing going on, too. I silently wondered if the other family members were dosed and eyed the perimeter of the deck for a tainted water source.

Some people were placed in the middle of the deck. Others were blindfolded and told that they were to walk across the deck without bumping into anyone else. If the walkers got too close, those standing were to push them away *with their auras*. This was a little much for me, having grown up in a church in which ritual was a cube of Wonder bread and a shot of grape juice. But I'll be damned if those people didn't make it across.

Pretty soon, I was caught up, too. I moved chairs and collated photocopies of scripts in the morning, then had afternoon rehearsals of plays in which I mostly played eight-year-olds or characters named MAN THREE. In the late afternoon, we had Playlab, which was a program for the apprentices. We wrote, acted, hung lights, and did touchy-feely drama exercises. The Playlab's playwright-in-residence was Vic Gilliam, whose name I recognized. He grew up a couple of blocks away from me, he was a few years older, and he was gay.

Vic cast me in his play as the gay guy who confesses an obsessive crush on his best friend and goes full-tilt boogie psychotic. I got to throw things and wield a knife, as well as smoke a prop joint rolled with what I think was oregano.

My infatuation with Jim had become obvious to nearly everyone in the company. Around midnight every night, the retreat director had to shoo me out to my car. It must have scared the bejesus out of Jim to be stalked by a sixteen-year-old. He avoided me as if I were a rabid squirrel.

Being in such proximity to Jim for two solid weeks meant that I sank deeper into my yearning, filling a two-hundred-page notebook before the retreat was over. I wrote poems, dialogue, and painfully detailed accounts of my obsession. An actor took me aside at one point.

"You write a lot," he said.

"Yeah."

"Writing's better than loving," he said. "You'll have something to show for your time. Stick to writing."

"What about writing *about* loving?" I asked.

"If you must," he said grandly, taking a three-second drag from his cigarette. "But take care of this," he said, placing a hand on my heart. His hand was freezing. "Don't get bitter. You're just a little puppy."

By the time we staged a reading of Vic's play, I'd memorized the entire thing. I dropped my script to recite the climactic two-page monologue which concluded with my character grabbing a knife. It was pure Garbo. The character reveals to his best friend that he's secretly in love with him and tells him how destructive it is to repress emotions. Then my character jams the knife into the wall. As a friend of mine says, I was *feeling the realness.*

The retreat director said he almost stopped the reading because I was "out of control." I think it was the first time I approached being half-decent on stage. Jim, wisely, missed my performance. He knew it would be all about him.

I continued to leave poems in Jim's mailbox. Rather than deal with me face to face, he mostly left notes. Talking to him only made it worse, and he knew it. Jim's last note said "Ever thought of trying to write a play?"

the convincing death

The proverbial theater bug is like a tick which makes itself fat and juicy on the youthful idealism of new converts. When I got home from the playwrights retreat, I had trouble relating to my friends. I'd spent two weeks with the carnival, and reentry into my old life was rough. I felt my heart jump right out of my body, and I learned there was nothing I could do about it, other than to let it wander.

An actor was leaving a local production of *King Lear* early, and Ms. Curtis asked me to replace him. Her husband Tom was directing it and they needed someone immediately. The fourth soldier had no lines, but he got to die right there on stage, night after night. At that point I would have sold candy bars and hot chocolate just to be near a theater.

Tom Curtis stirred me up the moment I met him. By that point, the whole crushing-out on my director motif was becoming an embarrassing schoolboy cliché, but I couldn't resist. My friend Eileen once said about Tom "I'd kick him out of bed—to fuck him on the floor."

A lot of the people at the theater were hippies. They smoked and drank and had kids from multiple marriages. After one evening backstage, I was certain that I would be in theater for the rest of my life.

The soldiers' costumes consisted of baggy black gypsy pants, a fabulous striped cotton belt, and a hat fashioned from a metal colander and camouflage netting. There was something post-modern going on, but I couldn't quite figure out what it was

At this theater, they did Shakespeare with a thick Appalachian accent. I had to stand on stage with a straight face as Lear's youngest daughter drawled through lines such as "What shall Cordelia do? Love, and be silent." Such an accent triples the number of syllables in any given word, so the play's running time was approximately eleven hours.

When I died, I tried not to drag it out to the point of being obnoxious. I took a direct stab, then scraped my feet across the dirt as I tried valiantly to walk away. But then I fell, making sure I got good lighting as I slumped to the ground. Tom, between puffs of his ever-present unfiltered cigarette, said I died convincingly.

The last night I died, I returned to the backstage area to re-arrange the netting on my colander. A broad-chested older man appeared in the doorway. He was in a black tee shirt and beat-up khakis. We exchanged pleasantries.

He told me he thought I was talented. I may have been naïve, but I was not *completely* stupid. Still, for an attention-hungry teenager, it was one hell of a hook.

"All I did was fall down. Any dumb-ass can do that," I said.

I didn't have any make-up to remove or else this would have been a perfect movie-queen-greeting-her-public sort of scenario. We talked further, and he gave me his number. Above the number, with curvy penmanship, he'd written the letter *J*. He said it stood for Jackson.

He told me to call anytime. He stressed that it didn't matter what time.

The following afternoon, I was recording myself playing a song I'd written on my guitar. Let's just say it was really earnest and leave it at that. Jackson said he'd gotten my number from infor-mation. I was intrigued as to why someone would go to such trou-ble. No one had ever looked me up before.

He asked what I was doing. He said I should play the song for him. So I did. When I finished, I picked up the receiver and asked what he thought.

"What do you have on?" he asked.

"What do you mean?"

"What are you wearing?"

"Shorts and a tee shirt—how come?"

"Why don't you take off the shirt?" he asked.

I froze.

"Did you take it off?" he asked.

I said yes even though I hadn't. He said he wanted to see how my body looked, that maybe some time we could get together so he could see. I didn't say anything else. He kept talking, telling me he was in his underwear and that he thought I was talented. He kept saying that. I put my guitar down and looked into the phone. I stared at the tiny holes where his voice came through. I stared at the sharp edges and touched them to see if they were sharp enough to cut my finger.

"I have to go now," he said.

I couldn't stop thinking about him. I called the next day and he asked me to come by that evening. When I arrived, his house was a total mess. There were paintings leaning against furniture and clothes stacked in heaps. It looked like he was moving.

We talked for an hour about theater, about my future, about this alleged talent of mine. I kept looking at the windows, even though all the shades were pulled. A few doors down the street was my piano teacher. A half block the other way was Rich's house. I'd been on this street hundreds of times before. How can someone live on a street so long without being noticed?

He asked me to take off my shirt. I did, then held it in a ball against my chest. He gently extracted it from my grip, then asked if I'd take off my pants. As I removed my shoes, he kneeled in front of me and pulled off my jeans. He kept his clothes on.

"Let me rub your back," he said. He motioned me onto the thick beige carpet, where I lay on my belly. He dragged his hands across my back, brushing more than rubbing. I wondered when he was going to ask me to go into the other room.

He sat back and took off his shirt and pants, then lay down next to me. I watched the fat gather around his middle and go flush with the floor.

"It's getting late," I said, not looking at him as I sat up. He disappeared into the bathroom, perhaps to spare himself the pain of watching me dress and leave.

As I turned the doorknob to go, I gave him a hug—a theater hug. He pressed his sweaty forehead to my ear and said in a stage whisper, "You'll be back."

Three months later, I was in a Richmond hotel, auditioning for a theater scholarship. My monologues were thoroughly inappropriate and poorly executed. The panel of judges stared at me without a trace of the knowing mercy I'd come to expect from high school teachers. I was *that* bad.

On the other side of the lobby, I saw Jackson. We both said hi and he immediately asked if I could go to his room to talk. I nodded and we rode the elevator to the fifth floor in silence.

The air in his room was bitter. On the dresser, a cigar stub stood crooked in a glass of watery scotch.

We kissed. His lips were thin and cold. He set his eyeglasses on the bedside table and lifted my shirt. He undressed both of us and we took turns laying on top of each other. When our underwear came off, he reached for me, then pulled back.

"We should stop," he said.

"Why?" I asked.

"We should stop because I hate how it feels after," he explained.

I guess I knew what he meant by "after." Rich and I always took turns going first each time we had sex.

"Okay," I said, getting dressed.

Once we'd replaced all of our skins, he hugged me tight and grabbed the hair on the back of my head.

"Be strong," he said. "You have to get help. You can change."

I stepped back from him.

"I'm fine," I said.

Then I drove home.

In Charlottesville, I stopped at a fast food place. I ordered a vanilla milk shake, large fries, and four regular roast beef sandwiches. I ate every single bit. I got the key to the bathroom from the cashier and locked myself in to get to the part we hadn't reached—the scary part, the after.

the talk

My junior year, I took my friends one by one for long drives on country roads to have "the talk."
They seemed genuinely interested, and it probably struck them as naughty and exotic. After the first few conversations, I was well-prepared for the usual questions, like "How long have you known?" and "Do your parents know?" The best question any of them ever asked me was "Does that mean you're going to live in New York City?"

"Oh, yes," I told her.

Often, I got lost during these excursions. I reassured myself that all roads eventually lead back to the county seat. With Johnna and Kate, the reaction was quick. "So what, I already knew, it's totally okay."

Girls tended to already know. In junior high school, I was the one who painfully, awkwardly tried to be as much like them as I could. As much, anyway, as I could get away with. Being gay gave me a special role at school. I seemed more trustworthy to the girls, more mysterious to the boys. I wasn't a boy or a girl. I was between them, a sort of gender diplomat. Girls had already told me their most intimate secrets and fears, so telling girls was easy.

With guys, I was a lot more nervous. When I got Neil in the car, I was well-practiced in the art of coming-out. I took him to the river, where we sat and talked for a solid hour before I began steering the conversation toward matters homo. Nobody can steer a conversation like a gay person. Like gaydar, it is one of our birthrights.

Neil was my first best friend. Our mothers met on one of Lexington's main drags, when the two of us were in strollers. Noting that we were three months and three blocks apart, our mothers decided that we would be regular playmates.

He and I walked to and from school together for years. We got in fights as a team and tormented Vicky Sweeton together. I turned him on to KISS. He introduced me to Dungeons and Dragons. We had a shared history that spanned our entire lifetimes. So much depended on Neil's reaction.

We sat on the roots of the tree that held the ropeswing, two feet from the road. Neil calmly listened as I sputtered through my rehearsed but nervous confession.

"Oh, man," he interrupted. "Let me give you a hug."

We sat against the tree in silence. Neil draped his arm across my shoulders.

Trucks with gun racks sped by us. They didn't seem to bother him. He didn't need to say anything else. I knew exactly where we were.

militerry

We got a new principal my freshman year. When she spoke to the entire freshman class in the band room, I tried like hell to cultivate an adversarial relationship with her. In front of everyone, I grilled her about the school policy on ripped jeans. With more vinegar than eloquence, I made a case for freedom of expression through clothing. The things principals have to endure. She heard me out, then invited me to meet with her after school to discuss it further.

I made a list of talking points before the meeting. She listened to me, then gave a commonsense appraisal of why ripped clothes were tacky and disruptive to learning. I didn't agree with her, but she had that tough Southern woman charm—Molly Ivins charm, Blythe Danner charm. I left her office feeling like I'd gotten more than I'd asked for, when actually I got nothing. After that, I wore my ripped jeans only on weekends. And Mrs. Terry always winked at me in the hall.

"You don't want to waste your energy on a silly thing like this, do you?" she asked as I was leaving. "Save that fight for something important."

The next time I had a meeting with Mrs. Terry, it *was* for something important.

I'd spent hours staring at photos of members of the AIDS Coalition to Unleash Power getting arrested and shaking their fists in the air. They wore combat boots and had rage on their faces. They were punks. They were smart. They were in New York.

I wanted to be with them, shutting down the FDA and harassing Jesse Helms. I wanted a rap sheet and a lawyer. I wanted to get in the faces of everyone who'd ever been mean to me and I wanted to scream until *they* were afraid.

Seeing as how I was sixteen years old and . . . um . . . struggling with algebra, the parameters of my revolution were meager. At the beginning of the year, every student was given a handbook that every student immediately trashed. But I never threw anything away, much to the chagrin of my mother. Dad was a pack rat, Mom was all about purging.

I read the handbook from cover to cover, looking for something that could lead to my political imprisonment. Something gay. Some horrible affront to my civil rights that I could bring to the attention of the global community. I had it all planned out, the way teenage daydreamers will do.

There would be reporters everywhere. For miles. In my mind, it was somewhere between Beirut and the Oscars.

On page fourteen, I found it. Under the dance rules and regulations: "A student shall not bring a member of the same sex to a school dance."

Oh, that was a good one. That could get me on *Donahue* and *Oprah*. I'd never heard of Aaron Fricke, so I didn't know that all the gay prom drama had been played out a decade beforehand. I immediately made an appointment with the principal.

I arrived promptly for my meeting with Mrs. Terry, who had earned the moniker "Militerry" from the more creative rank and file of our student body.

Again, I'd prepared talking points. I vowed that I would not be diverted by her considerable charm. But once I sat down, I stammered and sputtered like a three-year-old trying to read. My years in the debate club were completely useless. Finally I said, "Well, it's a dumb rule and I think you should change it."

Militerry was a total sport. "My sense of the rule," she told me, "is that it's designed to keep football players from bringing their buddies as dates."

Who were the football players doing *that?* I thought for a moment that there was indeed hope for my love life. I scanned the faces of the football team in a photo that hung on the wall behind her desk.

"They bring their friends from other schools, instead of going through the process of signing up guests ahead of time," she said, "and they get in for a dollar less as a couple."

"Well, what if I want to bring a guy to a dance?" I asked.

"Under this rule, you can't. But I honestly don't think they had your situation in mind when they made the rule. It was written a long time ago."

She didn't have the power to change the rule herself, because the rules fell under the jurisdiction of the school superintendent.

I went home and drank a steady stream of Diet Coke, getting myself wired far beyond obnoxious. I sat down at my computer and began typing what would become a three-page single-spaced letter. In it I outlined the grave constitutional violations of the rule and the damage it did to my civil rights. I used lawyer words because Wade, my boss from the record store, had taught me a million of them—*punitive, unmitigated, egregious.* I even threatened a lawsuit that would certainly bankrupt the county's school system. The details of this lawsuit were relatively vague since, beneath all this rhetoric, I didn't have the slightest clue what I was talking about.

But when you're sixteen, arrogance is gasoline. The gay rights movement would be a lot more interesting if sixteen-year-olds were drafting press releases and mission statements for political organizations. Teenagers, unaware of the indirect sludge that is politics, articulate exactly what they want.

My family's friend Tank had been over for dinner, and when I finished the letter, I raced downstairs to show it to him. I'd always loved shocking Tank, who was a devout Christian and military man.

He read the letter with a pen in hand. Halfway through the first page, Tank took a deep breath and set the pen on the table.

"This is going to be controversial," he said. "Do you really want to put yourself in that position?"

"Yes," I said immediately. Oh, baby! Now we're *talking*.

He finished the letter, then folded his hands in his lap.

"People are going to think you're a homosexual if you send this letter."

"I'm fine with that," I chirped, still buzzing from the Diet Cokes.

"That's all anybody will think of you. Do you want to be a single-issue person?"

We got into a heated argument, which delighted me. That meant the letter worked.

"I don't think you should threaten them," he said.

"I *love* that part!"

The next day I drove to the school board offices and delivered the letters: one addressed to the superintendent and one to the school board.

A week later, I received a letter in the mail from the superintendent

Dear Mr. Read,

I write in response to your letter to me dated November 6, 1989.

The intent of the regulation in the Lexington High School handbook of student conduct to which your letter refers was to bar undesirable non-students from attending school dances It is not the intent of the school board to discriminate on the basis of students' race, color, creed, national origin, handicap, or gender. After reviewing the regulation, I have determined that such a regulation might indeed lead to discrimination against certain students.

While it is still true that there are some non-students who are unwelcome at such functions, it will be necessary for this board to

find another method to prevent them from attending. A no-tres-
passing notice would be satisfactory.

The handbooks of student conduct are printed annually. At the
next printing, the regulation discussed above will be changed.

On one hand, I was thrilled that some higher-up had responded
at all. And I'd gotten what I asked for, right?

On the other hand, I was furious that this man's sensible toler-
ance had short-circuited my elaborate scheme that would, ultimately, have landed me in a chair opposite Barbara Walters. I
wanted cameras. I wanted to make dramatic speeches before the
school board. I wanted to leave the building in sunglasses, surrounded by huge bodyguards who held my elbows as they stuffed
me into the back of a black Lincoln. I wanted to be pelted with
Bibles as mobs of angry protesters burned the school the fuck to the
ground. This "we'll change it" letter was totally anticlimactic.

I'd worked myself into a dither telling friends about sending the
letter. When I showed them the response, they were far more
excited than I was. I felt as if I'd been in a tug-of-war, straining
and digging my heels into the ground. Suddenly, the other team
had let go of the rope.

I couldn't take Rich. He was out of college by that point and totally uninterested in going to a high school prom. Plus, it was
against the rules to take someone over the age of twenty-one
because they might buy alcohol for you. Which—*hello*—is half
the fun of knowing people over the age of twenty-one.

Our prom theme that year was "Stairway to Heaven." Did I
really need to subject a gay man to that anyway?

the **cure**

Vic's Manhattan zip code made him a thoroughly exotic creature. He'd not only escaped Lexington, but he was living in a gay ghetto. By the time Christmas rolled around, I'd finished my first play was ready to show it to him. I called his parents repeatedly to ask when he'd be home. They politely took messages and said he'd be home shortly.

The evening of December twenty-third, I broke Emily Post's rule of not telephoning before 9 A. M. or after 9 P. M.. Shortly before midnight, Vic answered my call with a three-syllable *hello*.

"You're home!" I screamed.

"I have a gift for you," he said.

I panicked. Raised the consummate Southerner, I subscribe to the rule that one never greets anyone empty-handed. I contemplated delaying our meeting so I could rush out the next morning and buy him an appropriate gift, but I couldn't wait to see what he'd brought me from New York City.

"How about *now?*" I blurted.

"Um, sure," he said. "I'll be right up."

I opened the door before Vic had a chance to knock and hugged him tightly. He handed me a large brown box. It read "Open in the privacy of your room."

"Come on," I said, leading him upstairs.

It was like that episode of *The Brady Bunch* in which Jan is feeling unspecial because she's the middle girl. Her crazy aunt shows up with gifts from India. I tripped going up the stairs but held the box above my head to shield it from damage.

"Cardboard isn't fragile," Vic said.

I closed the door and ripped the box open, then sat down in the middle of the floor. Inside was a stack of magazines, newspapers, and books. There was *Outweek*, the cover boy of which was closet-case Malcolm Forbes. There was *Out/Look*, a short-lived art and political magazine based in San Francisco. There was the *New York Native*, a radical gay newspaper with letters to the editor which could have been adapted into operetta. And there were two books—Edmund White's *A Boy's Own Story* and David Leavitt's *Family Dancing*.

I held them in my hands and ran my fingers across the spines. I felt the book covers, which gleamed like expensive dentistry. I rubbed the *Native*'s acidic newsprint pages, which stained my fingers gray.

That night, I read *A Boy's Own Story* in one sitting. I drank Diet Coke all night and took a couple of No-Doz around 4 A. M. so I could finish. I continued reading into the morning, finishing *Family Dancing* as well.

White's "about the author" page listed a book titled *The Joy of Gay Sex*. I knew I'd never find it at a local library or bookstore, and there wasn't one of those clip-out coupons in the back. A few days after New Year's, I drove eighty minutes to the University of Virginia library to search for it.

The card catalog sent me to a section next to books on drug addiction, prostitution, and child abuse. White's book wasn't in the stacks. I looked around, and seeing no one, proceeded to empty three shelves of books onto the floor. I was going to find that goddamn book.

Finally, I saw it. It was on the floor, wedged in between the support beams of the shelf. Someone more scared than I was had hidden it there. Maybe he had glanced at it late at night, then hidden it again.

I replaced all the books and scurried into the men's room. I picked the stall furthest from the entrance and closed the door. I sat down and didn't look up for two hours. The book was filled with explicit line drawings and encyclopedic descriptions of various sexual acts, most of which I had yet to enjoy.

Inside the stall, there were all sorts of entreaties scratched into the mustard-colored enamel paint. Phone numbers and bold personal statements filled the wall just above the toilet paper. Perhaps I might actually meet someone here who could guide me through everything I'd just learned. Now that I was book smart, I needed a benevolent stranger.

I waited for another two hours. Clandestine gay sex requires that one become fluent in the language of waiting. Every time the door opened, my breathing slowed to the point that I could hear the tile floor eroding beneath my feet. My armpits dropped beads of sweat, which tickled my sides and reminded me that I might not be ready for this, whatever *this* was.

He was around forty, I'd decided. He saw me through the crack in the stall door and winked the way teachers do when you're trying to be endearing. As I opened the door, he extended his hand to me and pulled me to his chest. He stroked my hair and kissed my forehead. He whispered in my ear, "Let's get out of here." I went home with him—home to his house full of gay books, home to his golden retrievers, home to his yard full of tomatoes, home to the bed which would become my classroom—and I never left.

No one showed up. It was midnight and outside I heard lights clicking off. I feverishly ripped the bar codes out of the book so that I wouldn't trigger the sensor gates on the way out of the library. I'd seen library clerks demagnetize books before by rubbing the spine across a black metal slab. The spine, too, had to go. It was full of alarms. I ripped the cover off altogether and shoved it into the trash can, then covered up the evidence with handfuls of paper towels.

I stuffed the book under my jacket and into the waistband of my pants. A friend and I had shoplifted hundreds of dollars worth of cassettes in the pockets of our camouflage pants, the covers of tennis rackets, and long shirt sleeves. I was a seasoned criminal, but I'd never stolen anything that mattered so much.

I took a deep breath as I approached the detector near the front door. It screamed. I heard a piercing metallic voice saying "Stop thief!" But it was just the machine, sounding two shrill notes of disapproval.

The clerk said, "Sir, could you bring your bag over here?"

I put my backpack on the counter.

"Could you open it for me? Maybe there's a book that didn't get scanned properly."

I was caught. I was going to jail for destroying a book. I'd only had one overdue library book in my entire life. As a child, I checked out dozens of books a week and always brought them back on time. The one exception was a young adult how-to book about spying and invisible ink and secret codes and low-level espionage. Two months after I paid for a replacement, the librarian called me to let me know they'd found it stuck in the book return slot.

The clerk, seeing no books, pulled out my Walkman.

"Whatcha listening to?" he asked.

"The Cure," I said.

"That sounds about right," he said, looking at the mound of hair that fell over my eyes.

Head on the Door," I continued, wondering if he would call city cops or just use campus police.

"Good record," he said.

"I don't have any books," I said, adjusting my stance so the book would slide further down my pants.

"It's probably the Walkman. Sometimes they set it off."

"Oh, yeah. Probably so," I agreed, shaking so hard I couldn't zip up the backpack.

"I've never seen you here," he said.

"I'm not from here."

"Okay. Well, get home safe," he said. "And try *Pornography.*"

I almost threw up.

"It's the Cure's best album," he explained.

I strapped on my pack and made my way to the door. The alarm sounded again and I walked past it quickly. I pushed the door open and stepped into the freezing January air.

vibrate

When I returned to school after Christmas break, it was time for me to present a semester's worth of writing for my junior year independent study.
After logging hundreds of hours at my desk, I wanted to play rock star. My addiction to people was seriously compromised by that brutal reality of writing—you have to sit there, alone, and poop until you're empty.

I bought a music stand and jumped around in front of my bedroom mirror, tossing poems I'd read to the floor. The only real models I had for this presentation were rock concerts. No one told me that ninety minutes was a good bit longer than a writer was supposed to hold court.

I cast a reading of my play *ropeswing* with the drama club kids, as well as my friend Neil, who hadn't acted much but had an instinctive understanding of the dialogue rhythms. I didn't sleep the night before and made copies at Wade's office.

I'd been to see our family doctor for chronic stomach pains several times that semester. I didn't have an ulcer yet, so he prescribed Tums, stress reduction, and no more Diet Coke. My mother remarked that when she was a child, there was no such thing as stress. Back then, she said, it was just called *life*. It's good that the doctor gave us multiple options, because stress and Diet Coke were not leaving my routine any time soon.

Perhaps unwisely, before and after the reading I played several songs I'd written. These were the only really stinky moments. The reading went well, and to the seventy-five people gathered in the school library, it was my official coming-out statement.

After the play, I stood up and began reading poems. I'd done time on our school forensics team, so I was used to the blank stares of an audience. I felt it was my responsibility to twist those faces into expressions of shock, bemusement, and sympathy. And I can only do that by emptying my guts.

For those forensics competitions, I did a dramatic interpretation of the scene in *Of Mice and Men* in which George shoots Lenny in the head to prevent him from being taken to prison. I played it as a homoerotic gesture of mercy from one lover to another. Before I pulled the trigger, I stroked Lenny's hair and kissed the back of his head. The judges gave me second and said, with raised eyebrows, "That's a *very* tough piece."

The girl who beat me was obviously the drama princess of her school. She did a scene from *I'm Not Rappaport*, featuring an old cranky man. Drama judges, for reasons unbeknownst to me, love seeing teenagers play very old people.

When we got to the state finals, a black girl did a monologue from James Baldwin's *Go Tell It On the Mountain* and buried us all. As she spoke, the whole room was vibrating.

I wanted to make the room vibrate. I was nervous in a useful sort of way; I jumped around and tossed off wildly inappropriate asides. I'd handed out copies of my play as well as a hundred-page chapbook of poetry titled *Monster*. Essentially, I was handing them a prettied-up stack of pages ripped from my diary.

The Colonel had always raised us with the adage "keep your own counsel," while my mother was a fan of spilling utterly intimate family anecdotes to complete strangers. Absent the opportunity to indulgently broadcast my life, I would have chopped up my wrists. Five minutes into my first reading, I realized why one's own adrenaline beats the hell out of someone else's sympathy.

That evening, when I went downstairs for dinner, there was a Bible sitting on the steps. Dad had marked it up in blue pen.

The margin-writ Bible has an enduring tradition in my family. My great-grandmother, Miss Kirkpatrick, left her husband in the 1920s. Dad later found the Bible her husband had marked. Thin red lines underscored every damning word my great-grandfather could find about the corrupting nature of Woman.

Dad said nothing that night about my play. He was still digesting the fact that I was coming out so decisively, and there was nothing he could do to stop it.

On my way upstairs, I thumbed through the Bible the Colonel had left for me. Every passage he'd marked was about the love of God. Love, no matter what.

Valerie was my emotional girlfriend. That's how she

signed the notes she'd pass me in eleventh-grade English, right
under the nose of Ms. Coffey. Luckily, if Ms. Coffey really liked
a student, they were beyond reproach. I can't count the hours I
spent after school, confessing to Ms. Coffey my every conceivable intimacy. When I came out to her in a fourteen-page essay
on Kate Chopin's *The Awakening,* she wrote a response in red ink
that filled almost as many pages. She gave me an A and let me get
away with murder for the rest of the year. God bless Ms. Coffey.

I think the major reason that she didn't intercept our notes was
that she could see that Valerie was a dyke in progress. Valerie was
loud. I mean, Valerie was *really* loud. She'd moved to Lexington
the year before, during our sophomore year.

Valerie had come to us from Mississippi, where she'd apparently had a lot of religion in her life. She was Baptist and heavily involved with Young Life, a Christian organization that takes
kids on camping trips for fireside indoctrination. Valerie actually lured me to one of their events, which was replete with
earnest teenagers singing Michael W. Smith songs and profess-
ing their love for Jesus. During the campfire circle everyone
started witnessing about Christ and testifying about how they'd
found their faith. These children were like *fifteen.* When they
got around to me, I said, "I'm not really into the God thing. I came

because Valerie told me we'd play lots of games." Valerie turned as white as the turtleneck she wore almost daily, with a gold cross that dangled between her not-there-yet breasts.

I left the circle shortly after several college students, in front of everyone, tried to save me with their dramatic tales of conversion. One young woman worked up tears as she recounted how she'd been brought to her knees by the Lord, whereupon I went back to my cabin. If God had to go to such lengths to invite people to his birthday party, I reasoned, He probably wasn't serving very good cake.

Valerie knew early on that I was gay and never tried to talk me out of it. She never even tried very hard to convert me. This was not the case with all of her friends. Once, she caused a major scene during Christmas at her best friend Kate's house. The Crenshaw family was not much for organized religion, good hippies that they were. Valerie pointed at their baby Jesus ornament and demanded that they take it down. Valerie said that unless they were Christian, they had no business putting the baby Jesus on their tree. A long discussion ensued, followed by Valerie spinning their driveway's gravel with the tires of the car which had come to be known as the "Blue Blur." Valerie was known as the fastest Christian in Rockbridge County.

So it came as somewhat of a surprise when Valerie sat me down for her lesbian confession. We were at our friend Gresham's house, where all of us hung out compulsively, watching the same movies repeatedly. She said my play had made her question her own sexuality.

"That's awesome," I said.

I mean, there were signs, but her Baptist shit had me confused. Valerie had yet to teach me the remarkable similarity between a born-again Christian and a militant lesbian. She was always the first to instigate fights with the West Virginia soccer teams we played, which were often composed of massive, violent boys who'd been rejected by their football teams. It would have behooved Valerie to be more afraid of these boys. Valerie rarely did what was in her best interest.

That weekend, we drove to Roanoke, an hour south, to see Philip Kaufman's *Henry and June* in a tiny armpit of a theater. The movie is about the lives of Henry Miller, Anaïs Nin, and a gaggle of French writers and bohemians. Many cigarettes are smoked, much nookie occurs. I knew that seeing the film would be a different kind of conversion experience for her. When we arrived, there were maybe six people in the entire theater. Because I'd already seen the movie, I got to watch Valerie lay eyes on Uma Thurman for the first time, and I got to see her eyes utterly cross as she saw two women make love. I whispered in her ear that I was going to check her seat cushion after the movie. She smacked my arm.

On the drive home, Valerie chain-smoked Camel Lights, ranting about Uma Thurman. Unwisely, I had let her drive. This was a dangerous enough proposition under ordinary circumstances, but given her sensory overload, we were a pair of crash test dummies waiting for our brick wall to arrive.

I was thrilled to have a partner in all of this homo-splendor. If there is safety in numbers, two beats the hell out of one. And Valerie, with her born-again vigor, would more than double the openly homo population at Lexington High School.

Valerie's seductive charms were not entirely lost on me, despite the fact that we were on different sides of the gender highway's double yellow lines. Even though she'd begun her pursuit of full-fledged dykehood, she was still very active at the Faithful Shepherd Baptist Church. A new youth minister named Grant had been hired to invigorate the sizable youth group, which was the envy of every church in town.

Valerie had managed to get a lot of butts in the church's seats. Most of my friends attended the performance, where Grant, in clown makeup, did sappy pantomime skits to Harry Chapin's "Cat's in the Cradle" and a few songs with messages along the lines of We Love Jesus, Yes We Do, We Love Jesus How 'Bout You?

We all squirmed in the pews as the youth minister pranced around, busting interpretive dance moves.

My Methodist father was immediately suspicious that I would be brainwashed by the Baptists. Dad had turned bright red when I attended a few Catholic youth events earlier in my junior year. Dad was still bitter that the Catholics had kept things in Latin for so many years. He didn't care much for the concept of priests, either. "Priests are middlemen," he said. "Go direct to Christ."

But the Baptists were throwing the best parties in town. They held lock-ins and camping trips and scavenger hunts. I was in the Methodist vocal and handbell choirs, so I couldn't go to the Baptist church on a regular basis anyway. I had graduated from acolyte to usher and continued to attend Sunday school. This had everything to do with our Sunday school teacher, on ecumenical loan from the youth-starved Lutheran church. I thought he was adorable. He allowed us to choose our topics of discussion, so my friend Christine and I were constantly suggesting homosexuality, abortion, satanism, and the death penalty—the good stuff.

On the third Sunday of every month, Valerie and I were booked to play during the offertory at her church. I brought in my twelve-string guitar and we sang Indigo Girls songs as they took up collection. The blue hairs were beside themselves with glee, apparently unaware that we were two queers singing songs by two queers. During the most surreal moment, when we sang the line "I stopped by the bar at 3 A. M. to seek solace in a bottle or possibly a friend," I could see our friend Toby Higgins sitting on the front row, mouth agape. Still, after the service, Valerie and I were mobbed by happy Baptists.

"Y'all are just so dern *precious!*" they'd coo. Valerie and I were planning to sing "Hey Jesus" one Sunday, which details a dumped lesbian lover's ensuing doubts in God. But we pulled back on that one, knowing that getting away with it requires a certain maintenance of subtlety.

The youth minister, huddled us up one Sunday morning, suggesting that we form a traveling drama group. We'd have professional lighting, makeup, and props. We'd have rehearsals, public performances, and a repertoire of plays. Valerie and I quickly agreed. We gathered up several of our friends to fill out the group to seven. We started rehearsal that week.

The only person I didn't already know was a husky-voiced girl named Wanda from Buena Vista, (pronounced *BYOONA vista* and commonly referred to as B.V.). She and I did a skit together in which I strapped an enormous log to my head to illustrate the popular "stick in your eye, speck in someone else's" proverb. It was a big hit with the Christians we met on the road.

Grant had me learn an evangelical monologue. I was so excited to have ten minutes alone onstage that I didn't even question all the fever-pitched screaming. People would come up to me afterward and say it "brought the Lord to life." I just wanted to be an actress.

Valerie and I were constantly winking at one another during rehearsals, fully aware that we were freaks in a hilarious born-again sideshow. She was the bearded lady, and I was the sword swallower, only no one talked about that.

That spring, Grant gathered about twenty-five kids to put on a musical titled *Surrender*. All of the script's references to Lakewood High were changed to Lexington High because he said it would make God's message more meaningful to our audience. "It'll bring it home," he assured us. The songs had beautiful harmonies, so it was great fun as long as I held my nose about the lyrics. Some of the choice words I had to sing were

I'd rather go to Africa, than Lexington High
And give my testimony like a fool.
Bein' a believer isn't cool, oh no.
Bein' a believer isn't cool.

I had to hit an unreachable high note at one point, and everyone pretty much closed their eyes and prayed for it to be over. My mother's reaction to the performance was her standard line after voice recitals: "I'm glad this is fun for you, honey."

Meanwhile, I was falling for the musical director, who had a rat tail which, thankfully, he kept tucked beneath his shirts. I wrote sappy poems and lyrics for him, which I hand-copied in awkward blue ink and left in his church mailbox. They weren't explicit love poems, per se, but were chock-full of goopy references to him "helping me find my voice" and being an "angel." Dad was right. The Baptists *were* brainwashing me.

The following week, Grant and the music director stopped me in the hall. They said I would need to become a full member of the church in order to continue coming to youth activities.

"What," I asked, "is involved with becoming a member?"

"It means getting baptized, completely washed of sin," Grant said, "and making a commitment to live without that sin."

He was speaking the queen's English. My poems had rattled our music director, and they'd decided to root out the fag, or at least try to convert me.

"By baptism, you mean what?" I asked.

"Full immersion."

I envisioned a riverside scene featuring white robes, mud, a full gospel choir, and a minister dunking me backwards as water shot up my nose.

"I'm *so* not interested in that," I said.

"Then you can't be in the group," Grant said. "Think it over. You can change your mind."

After the final performance of *Surrender,* we had a meeting to discuss the future of the drama group. Grant had reached a decision that all non-Baptists in the group had to join the church. Of the seven members, five of us were from other churches.

"Can we vote on this?" I asked.

"No, this has come down from the board of the church. If you want to be in the drama group, you need to become a member."

"But I'm already baptized," I argued.

"You need to become a member of *this* church," he said.

What we weren't talking about, of course, was the washing-free-of-sin-and-living-free-of-sin part of the baptism. In other words, as long as I wasn't openly queer and agreed to go underwater, I could stay.

Samantha, another member of the group, was raised Catholic and was even more prissy about river mud than I was. So I knew she wasn't down with this.

"Then I'm out," I said.

Valerie started raging on Grant, telling him it wasn't right to force kids to get baptized. She ominously referred to a group walkout and raised her voice until she was standing up, face to face with him.

Christine and Samantha zipped their backpacks and stood up.

Valerie was still in his face, screaming at him about how he was driving everyone away and that he wasn't a real Christian if he did that.

Another group member stood up and walked out.

Wanda was the only one who hadn't said anything.

"Where are you on this, Wanda?" the youth minister asked.

"It ain't right," she said. Everybody hushed up. Even the born-again B.V. girl was walking.

Valerie looked at me and raised her eyebrows. We grabbed our backpacks and walked toward the door.

"If you change your minds, call me," Grant said. "We'll start a new group."

By this point, we were all halfway down the hall. He was left alone, surrounded by cheesy Bible-skit props.

In a pathetic pleading voice, he said, "Think about it, okay, guys?"

But we were all out the door. Without queers, there would be no more drama at the Faithful Shepherd Baptist church.

While Dad was relieved that my affiliation with the Baptist church had drawn to a close, he wasn't thrilled with the news of its successor. The three of us were crowded around our tiny wooden kitchen table eating dinner when the phone rang. Dad always finished his meals five minutes before Mom and I. Mom nagged him incessantly about the hiatal hernia he was sure to induce. He'd counter that in the military, one ate fast. The way he made it sound, if one didn't finish supper inside of thirty seconds, the communists would confiscate the remaining food.

Mom handed me the phone, saying it was someone from Richmond. A theater person, she thought aloud. It was Douglas Vandenberg, from New Stages Theater. My play *ropeswing* was one of five which had won a young writers contest for that year and he wanted to know if I'd come live in Richmond that summer while the company staged it.

The whole concept of parental permission was alien to me. I always said yes, then figured out how I could talk my parents into it. I hadn't even told them I entered the contest, because it never occurred to me that I had a chance at winning.

I had written the play really only to impress Jim, but Ms. Curtis urged me to pop it in the mail to the contest. Had there been even a five-dollar reading fee, I wouldn't have bothered. Why pay for rejection?

Douglas said there would be a real production with real actors and real lights and real sets. As I hung up the phone, I jumped up and down so hard that water sloshed out of our dog Thatcher's bowl.

Dad started at Hell No. I'd have to skip creative writing camp at the University of Virginia. Dad was convinced that the UVA admissions office would record this affront and block my application altogether. Dad muttered about me being a "single-issue voter," obliquely referring to the play's gay theme. I left Mom in the kitchen to lobby him and went upstairs.

Two hours later, I heard my father screaming "Cocksuckers!" over and over. Mom responded in a shrill burst of language that I couldn't untangle. Then she started banging pots and pans together. *That* I could understand. I grabbed a pen and my notebook and raced downstairs. This was going to be good.

I sat on the radiator in the corner of the kitchen and, like a court reporter, wrote down every word they said. This didn't seem to faze them. Even Dad had accepted that living with a writer guarantees scrutiny.

Dad was really drunk by then. He must have pounded a lot of scotch during the fight. He was an old school social drinker, and I only saw him visibly drunk a few times. I only saw him nasty drunk twice. This was the last time.

He was standing in the corner, sermonizing about gays in the military. Then the rhetoric swerved again.

"They're *cocksuckers!*"

Mom threw a frying pan into the sink and screamed, "*DUH!*"

"Let's use nineties language," Dad said. "It's not natural. What about *Life. God. AIDS.* Get the *facts straight!*"

Boyfriend was in his own little world. When I tried to argue with him, Dad banged the cookie jar lid, so all we heard was porcelain about to break.

Dad rattled on for another forty-five minutes with occasional interruptions from Mom. He talked about war, children, and his failure as a father. He talked about alligator-infested waters and men dying in his arms on Pork Chop Hill.

Mom and I were both lost. Dad started rambling about his military career. It was the only time I ever heard him explain why he hadn't made general. A young private, exhausted, landed his plane without lowering the wheels. The army was making an example of him. Dad defended him in military court and ended up throwing a well-known general's grandson through a door. Needless to say, he didn't progress beyond colonel.

"What does that have to do with homosexuals?" Mom barked.

"Don't you *see?*" he said, deflated.

"No," she said. "Explain."

"I did the same thing for homosexuals in the 1940s, in military court. I defended those people," he said, pointing randomly around the room. "I *fought* for them."

His finger never landed on me that night, but I knew exactly what was happening. My parents were having "the talk" about their youngest son. Dad started out spitting fire and brimstone, but after an hour, he was lamenting the departure of his children. He felt like he'd lost some of his kids to resentment and he knew that he was dangerously close to losing another. Mom and I saw the sadness in his wrinkled brow. We took seats at the table and watched him sputter like an untied balloon.

I was furious at first, but just sat and listened. The more I heard, the more I could see that Dad was just throwing a tantrum. Dad knew that going to Richmond would change me forever. As he continued screaming and ranting incoherently, Mom reached over and took my hand. Dad needed to get this out of his system. Then we could move on.

Finally, Dad ran out of words. He stood behind me and put his hands on my shoulders, then kissed the top of my head. Mom looked relieved. The three of us were a Norman Rockwell tableaux, painted in day-glo colors.

"*'DUH!'*" I said to Mom, "That was my favorite part of the whole fight."

The three of us started laughing. For good measure, Mom reached into the sink and dropped the frying pan again. As she sat back down, she grabbed the end of my pen and said, "You're going to make me cute and adorable, aren't you?"

Douglas drove to Lexington the last week in April to meet with me. He was visiting the five festival playwrights in our respective hometowns. When I saw him at the back gate, I knew instantly that a summer in Richmond would beat the hell out of two weeks at UVA's creative writing camp. My parents spotted him over the brick wall and Dad announced, "Your director's here."

Douglas was clad in all black, with rock star cowboy boots. Dad immediately offered him a drink. Before we could even start talking, Dad whisked Douglas away for a tour of the backyard. I watched them from the patio, praying that the Colonel wouldn't ask prying questions that would mortify me.

Somehow, Mom had convinced my father that Richmond was a good idea and that he needed to stop behaving as if I was being shipped off to Jonestown. When he and Douglas returned, they were giddy, swapping stories about the Civil War. Douglas had told my father that he was writing a musical about the Civil War, which pretty much sealed the deal. Dad was suddenly his biggest fan.

I took Douglas to the Maury River, where I'd written much of the play. I showed him the rope swing and read to him from my journal. Our conversation was magical. He'd read the play a dozen times and quoted lines back to me. He said he loved my voice and made references to a host of playwrights and novelists I'd never read. I took notes as he talked, writing down names such as Eugene O'Neill, Lanford Wilson, and Tennessee Williams. He made me promise him that I would read everything I could find by Williams.

Before we drove back, Douglas and I sat quietly on rocks at the river's edge. I was writing a poem and he was making notes to give to the set designer. He made notes about the color of the water, the posture of leaning trees and the sound of a distant waterfall, a mile downstream. I studied him as he stood and paced around the river bank. He seemed completely possessed by the play. It already sounded like he'd spent more time with it than I had. I knew instinctively that I could trust him with it. He turned, then said he thought I would be famous someday. This puzzled me, because I'd only written things down to keep from going crazy. The only time I'd ever been famous was when I was dancing in front of my bedroom mirror.

All five of us playwrights went to Richmond in May for company auditions. Dozens of actors were trying out for our plays. It was the first time I'd heard professional voices behind my words, and it was completely intoxicating.

Troy, one of the other playwrights, had also written a coming-out play, but he grew up Catholic, so there were a lot of long, rage-filled monologues. It's the first time I was ever grateful for being a Methodist.

That night, the three male playwrights camped out in sleeping bags on the floor of the theater office. Lonnie, Troy, and I were too excited to sleep. We talked about how writing had set us apart from our schoolmates and what a relief it was to be around other scribbling freaks. All day, actors and directors had fussed over us like we were royalty. But this was the thing—they weren't treating us like overachieving children, they were treating us like writers.

We compared notes on who we wanted in our plays. Troy and I talked about how strange it was to see straight actors auditioning for gay characters, especially when they didn't have the slightest idea how to approach it. In Troy's play, the two gay characters kiss, so this was a big deal to him. It was the first time I'd ever been able to talk with a gay guy who was my age. Troy and I allowed ourselves to lisp and coo and squeal without worrying about what anyone would think. For the first time, we were the majority. We graded guys we'd seen that day at auditions, then dropped them one full letter grade if they were straight and two full letter grades if they were straight *and* cute.

"What a waste of a good dick," Troy said. This startled Lonnie.

"*Everyone* in theater is gay," Lonnie said, breaking his silence. "Gay, gay, gay! It feels really weird to be straight." Then he farted, and the three of us broke into slumber-party giggles.

I'd been given advice on how to "dress for camera." Notably, I was supposed to avoid red, orange, and white. Stripes of any kind, I was told, would make the camera jump. This piqued my interest, because my bold-faced aim was to make the TV cameras in Richmond, Virginia, jump.

We five young playwrights from all over Virginia huddled around a series of wooden platforms which had been set up at New Stages for the filming. Sandy and Lonnie were tittering, ecstatic that they were going to be interviewed on TV. I wondered when Lonnie would sneak in his "Hi, Mom" moment. Keisha, the only black girl among us, was characteristically shy, far too young to know that her segments would be carefully edited to make the rest of us look less white. Troy and I were the only skeptical parties in the bunch. We strategized together about how to get the TV people to let us say the word *gay*.

The press about my play up until that point had been abundant but uneven. I'd been profiled for a piece in my local paper. In a tiny town, phrases like "sexual awakening" and "coming to terms with his sexuality" were sufficiently clear. This vague, Southern Gothic handling of sexuality was enough for Lexington, where everyone would hear the gossip before reading the article anyway. Articles that had been written so far in Richmond were also wispy about naming homosexuality, except for a few articles in the two local alternative papers.

It's ironic that I was so adamant about the word *gay* since I'd written a coming-out play that didn't invoke the word a single time. This was how people talked in Lexington. Everything was reduced to euphemism and genderless descriptions like *special someone* or, if they were really liberal, *significant other.*

But this was TV in the state capital. Troy and I were hell-bent on framing the discussion ourselves. The other three plays had themes we knew would be heavily featured. Sandy and Keisha wrote about troubled teens, peer pressure, and suicide—marketable, acceptable to advertisers, and easily described. The show's producers would come off looking like they'd tackled important teen issues. I could hear the lead-in already. Lonnie's play, on the other hand, was an oddball Brechtian farce about economic oppression, in which God is a brutal factory owner rendered, naturally, with a voice-over. The TV people would have *zero* idea what to do with that. Troy and I knew they couldn't gloss over the two of us.

A heavily made-up interviewer named Gretchen approached us with her hand outstretched. I was an arrogant little brat from that moment on. Her crew attached microphones to everyone's shirts and the interviews started.

I went last and knew from the other interviews that I had thirty seconds to speak, out of which, I figured, the producers would use about five. I said my central character's father comes out as gay, and when I used that word, the interviewer visibly flinched. At that point I looked directly at the camera and said, "And that's when the central character realizes *he's gay too.*"

The festival producer put her face in her hands.

"That's why we have editors," Gretchen said.

Later, when we had solo interviews, Gretchen tried to steer me toward discussing the play as a "coming-of-age drama." I must have said the word *gay* fifty times, refusing to give her usable footage that would allow her to paint the play as some sort of one-act *Stand By Me.*

Every time she got me started on a safe sound bite, I made fart noises in the middle of my sentence.

"You're not being cooperative," she said.

"I want to be honest," I said.

"This is for television," she said.

"Exactly," I said. "Think about all the gay kids out there."

She unclipped my microphone.

When the piece aired, the sexual awakening clichés won out. They used her voice-over for the gay bits. But you could still manage to tell what was going on. And the kids watching it, who had been well trained in decoding murky undertones, would get it.

Later in the month, the station aired my entire play, which shocked the hell out of me. I still wonder who made that decision. In my most idealistic daydreams, it was Gretchen.

action figures

Writing had been such a private act for me, but ever since rehearsals for the staging of <u>ropeswing</u> started, I'd lost my nerve. I became completely neurotic about being alone. In public, I was somewhat assured that if the page opened its jaws and swallowed me, there would be witnesses. Even if they couldn't save me, they'd know how I'd disappeared.

With pitiful Bambi eyes, I sat at the window of a coffee shop in Richmond, gazing out at passersby. Stacks of paper covered the table.

An older man always sat at the other window, reading enormous biographies, the kind that fall from high bookshelves during earthquakes and give people concussions. Every day, he had a new one—Nureyev, Paul Robeson, FDR. Our respective alcoves were visible to each other through a doorway. Sometimes I'd look up from my scribbling to see him gazing at me with curious concern.

A week went by. From our tables we went about our 9 A. M. routines. I averaged three Diet Cokes per visit, while he drank a single cup of coffee, black. It was Thursday, and the freeze date on my rewrites of the play was approaching. The night before, Douglas, the director, had pitched a characteristic tantrum, objecting to the stage manager's insistence that the cast have two solid weeks with a completely stable script.

I asked the cast if they would settle for two hours with a completely stable playwright. But it was beside the point, because they weren't getting either.

Our stage manager was perhaps the perfect counterbalance to Douglas's tempestuous directing style. She was an anal retentive who perpetually kept a pencil behind her ear to ensure that no T would ever go uncrossed. She constantly reminded us that very shortly the play would have a paying audience.

"It's about the words," Douglas screamed.

"It's about putting those words on stage," the stage manager retorted.

"That's *your* job," Douglas said.

"No, hon," the stage manager said, plopping down in her chair. "That's *your* job."

And then it got worse.

My twenty-four-page one-act had mushroomed into a fifty-six-page epic. That night, scenes were not working. The straight actor playing the gay boy was struggling. Douglas assigned him to numerous hours of Gay 101 with me, where he would mimic my expressions and intonations.

Douglas was a big brilliant kid, fingerpainting with the emotional lives of actors. There were two factions of Richmond actors—those who camped out like Springsteen fans for Douglas's auditions, and those who, having worked with him once, vowed never to do so again. The guru/monster dichotomy is often unavoidable in theater—to get those spurts of genius which cause theatrical cities to spring up and tickle the stars, one sometimes has to deal with someone like Douglas the Terrible.

The previous weekend, he'd packed the entire cast off to Lexington, where we had a full rehearsal by the river. He wanted the actors to touch the rope swing and feel the water of the Maury River on their ankles. Ever since the trip, the cast had hit a much deeper understanding of the play. They were getting the language, and that had everything to do with Douglas's often abrasive ability to insist.

I stayed up until two or three every morning, rewriting scenes entirely. At 7:30 A. M. every morning, we were due at the rehearsal space for a full-company aerobics session. Douglas had a dance background, so we all struggled through kicks, spins, and arty calisthenics. The beginning of every class started with Madonna singing "You can *dance!*"

"No I *can't,*" I'd shout back.

Despite my operatics, I couldn't wiggle out of aerobics. Nothing makes a diva angrier than a rule without exceptions.

I'd lobbied our dorm mother Sophia, who changed the spelling of her name every time she was in a play. She burned incense, read our astrological charts, and turned our attention to *Jonathan Livingston Seagull* every time we got too frustrated. Despite all her New Age shenanigans, she took a hard line on aerobics. I wasn't getting out of it.

I'd been crying almost every day, usually after rehearsal, but also in the mornings. It helped. There was a fat man I saw every morning before I went to the coffee shop. I'd follow him into Burger King and watch him eat two sausage biscuits. He was around fifty years old and got whatever action figure they were offering that day. He'd stand it next to his orange juice, then move it around the table, talking to it and making gun noises.

"Pow! Pow! Pow!"

He looks so innocent, I thought, but who loves him? Who can love a crazy person? I was starting to understand insanity, and every morning, I'd sit and wonder *will anyone love me when I'm playing with action figures?*

I'd sit in the corner of Burger King, watching him, emptying myself of whatever poison I'd accumulated from the previous night's rewrites.

Later, after my third Diet Coke at the coffee shop, I gave the table several solid head butts. When I looked up, the man who read biographies was sitting in front of me.

He pushed a bagel across the scattered pages.

"You need to eat something," he said.

"I don't know what the hell I'm doing."

"Well," he said, "the first thing to know is that banging your head is not helpful."

He pointed to a scar on my forehead.

"Opening old wounds?" he asked.

"You have no idea," I said.

"Actually, I do."

"I have to finish this play by tomorrow, and the whole thing sucks shit."

"You'll finish when you finish," he said. "It's a new play. You could hand actors a new scene on opening night. It's been done before."

"But I want to be finished," I said.

"A play is never really finished," he said.

This was not remotely comforting, although I'm sure he meant for it to be.

"How do you know?" I asked.

"Because I've written them."

"Not even *kinda* finished?" I asked.

"Kinda."

"It's a mess," I whined.

He told me how he'd written a play that almost went to Broadway. "So much depends on lunches," he said, a little sadly. "Why don't you read me what you have?"

We sat on a bench across the street from the coffee shop and I read the entire play to him. It was the first time I really heard it.

"How'd you know I was writing a play? I mean, before you came over to talk to me?"

"I saw your picture in the paper," he said. Then he extended his hand for me to shake. "I'm Walker."

On the Fourth of July, I skipped the company trip to an amusement park. I had more rewrites to do but secretly hoped I would run into Walker at the coffee shop. We'd become friendly over the past few weeks, talking for hours on end. I read to him from my writing, he read to me from whatever he was reading. He'd bring in books with sticky notes marking relevant passages he thought might ease my anguish. We read aloud to each other in the window of the coffee shop as people walked by.

I took him to the theater to show him the set for my play, which was a raked circular stage, an odd structure symbolizing a tree, and a rope dangling from the rafters. We sat in total darkness. I nervously rattled on about the set and how suggestive it was, how it was stark and poetic and how that suited the play and how much I loved it when the dappled blue lights cast shadows on the edge of the stage and all kinds of other bullshit that young writers go on about. Then I blurted out my confession.

"I was hoping I'd run into you this morning," I said.

He was breathing softly and let out something of a sigh. "Me, too."

Then nothing. I hate long silences when people are getting ready to say or do something momentous. I'm always afraid I'll burp or fart or say something completely inappropriate just to fill up the space.

On the armrest, our fingers touched, just barely. We both jumped back, like we'd been shocked by someone walking across carpet in thick wool socks. Then our fingers met—our pinkies. We held them there, gradually letting our palms touch. For hours, we sat in that dark theater, holding hands.

Later on, we lay in the grass between the theater and the cafeteria. In the distance, we could hear Fourth of July fireworks that sent flashes of orange into our piece of the night sky. The sky popped again, and we saw part of a green explosion disintegrate into dust. We kissed with our eyes wide open and I couldn't wait to tell my mother about him.

reckless

Closing night was complete chaos. The lobby was filled with well-wishers, including lots of friends from Lexington. Several were good old boys. I expected nothing less than pious horror, maybe even walk-outs. But they surrounded me afterward, saying "Fuckin' A!" and "Hell, yeah!" One girl said, "I don't understand it, but I think a lot of you." My parents loved it—even my father—but said they hoped my next play wouldn't use the F-word quite so much.

I drank champagne all night, hating the taste but feeling that I should drink champagne. When the party moved from the theater to the Blue & Gray Grill, I worked my way through the tightly packed crowd. A critic said I reminded him of Chekhov. I had no idea what that meant but, being Southern, I just smiled and said, "Thank you so *much*." People were rustling my hair and smacking me on the butt. A few tried to actually talk to me, but it was loud and I was too drunk to stand in one place very long. Some of them were actors who said they wanted to "work together."

"Excuse me," I said, "I feel throw-uppy."

I made my way back to the bathroom and splattered the urinal with vomit. During my third heave, Wade appeared at the doorway. He massaged my shoulders as I puked, then handed me a glass of water. There were chunks and mucous strings all over my shirt. I washed my face, then looked in the mirror. I wanted to throw up again. This was the worst, most stereotypical writer behavior. My family did so much drinking and drugging that surely I could just skip that phase. Douglas had given me several scary books about writers, such as Tennessee Williams's *Memoirs,* in which he's so fucked-up he can barely type. As I looked into the mirror, I could see myself fifty years from then, a spaced-out queen in plaid pants, smoking a strange little cigar, walking a strange little dog.

I blew my nose and cleared my throat, hocking up tangy post-puke spit. I vowed that I would avoid public puking, cocaine, and plaid pants.

I turned to Wade. "Someday I'm going to be really boring," I told him.

"Okay," he said. "You're allowed."

A week after my play closed, Walker and I took off for a weekend on one of Virginia's coastal islands. My head was completely spun. The island was quiet. The only thing Walker and I heard were seagulls and each other's voices. We read plays to each other, took walks on the beach, and waited on blankets for the sun to melt. It was always too overcast for a sunrise or a sunset, which we took as a dismal omen for our relationship.

The whole weekend was chock full of melodrama. We broke up, then got back together, then broke up, then got back together. His insecurities ran deep and would continually resurface throughout our relationship.

I would grow up and leave him behind, he said. I would find other people. I would disappear into the vastness of the world. Through no fault of their own, he reasoned, the young are incapable of genuine commitment. As soon as I escaped Lexington, I would find myself surrounded by vultures.

That weekend and in hundreds of letters over the next two years, I mapped out our future together. I envisioned the house where we'd live together. I named our dogs and cats. I alphabetized our bookshelves and divided household chores. But he had a point. I still had a year of high school and four years of college ahead of me. Five years was a very long time to live separately, and maybe I *was* too young for this sort of relationship.

In theory, we'd freak out one at a time, so that the other could be stable and comforting. Things quickly got histrionic, alternating between soulfully passionate and chaotically emotional. In many ways, I was too young for what was going on. But Walker was much older, and he didn't strike me as being any better equipped.

On Saturday night, we drove into Norfolk and tried to go to a gay bar called the Dock. The doorman took one look at me and said, "Nah, huh-uh." Then he looked at Walker and made a catty comment about "youngsters." Walker was humiliated, and I wanted to torch the place. When we reached the car, I tried to calm him by pointing out that the person who'd turned us away lacked front teeth.

We just needed to be in a room full of gay people. We needed to be in a place where we could hold hands without people staring. For two months, our relationship had remained a carefully guarded secret because of our age difference. I still wasn't legal. He could have been fired, evicted from his apartment, and sent to prison.

We walked the beach that night, tripping over the wooden dividers that landowners placed between their beachfront plots.

The next night we did something that I don't recommend for any couple who's having even the slightest bit of turbulence. We went to see James Taylor.

We held hands under our coats so people around us wouldn't see. I had no issue with public display of affection. My response to anyone who had a problem with seeing two men being tender was a big punk fuck-you.

Walker was much more demure about this, paranoid even. The only times I saw him totally relax was when we were in New York. There we held hands in the theater. He'd even bring my hand up to his mouth for a kiss. Our favorite moments were when the lights fell, just before the beginning of a play. We'd bump our heads together for a quick kiss, squeezing our hands together on the armrest, unhidden.

At the end of the James Taylor concert, we got into the car to return to Richmond. It was close to midnight and I was driving my mother's station wagon. We screamed at each other for half an hour, then made up, then fell even deeper in love. We agreed that we were meant to be together. Halfway to Richmond, I unzipped my pants and pulled Walker's head into my lap.

Referring to the writing mantra he'd drilled into my brain, I said, "Show, don't tell."

I cranked the stereo, which was playing Pink Floyd's "Comfortably Numb." I yeehawed and banged on the steering wheel. I love reconciliation.

That's when I heard the siren. Luckily, we had just enough time to get ourselves together. When the officer asked me why I thought he'd stopped me, I said in an affected drawl, "I don't have *no* idea."

Walker let out a high-pitched peal of laughter and the officer wrote me up for reckless driving. I was doing eighty-seven in a sixty-five.

The judge took away my license for three months. Dad was the chairman of the Virginia Highway Safety Commission. He said my spotty driving record already embarrassed him.

I wanted to tell him that it could have been a lot worse.

admissions

The week before I started my senior year, Mom and I went north to visit colleges. I hated Yale. I hated the pretentious admissions tour. I hated the rain-soaked concrete. And I hated the bitchy little gargoyles that clucked their fat tongues at me from the façades of the buildings. Most of all, I hated not being in the same room as Walker. He was the one who was pushing me to apply. He believed that the Yale School of Drama would put me on a fast track to Broadway, which was, in his mind, the pinnacle of any career in theater. I just wanted a boyfriend.

Before the campus tour, there was a perfunctory question-and-answer period. I already knew this game. My father had accompanied me on a tour at the University of Virginia the previous spring and had shown his gregarious, plaid pants-wearing ass by asking cheeky questions and flirting with the female admissions director, as he did with every woman who ever crossed his path. He was always able to do this without seeming at all slimy, and everyone in the world found him unbelievably charming. But he was my father, so I wanted to dive under the seat. A few other parents asked questions about the engineering school, computers in rooms, and campus police. Dad stood up and said something about regular report cards and cocktail parties for parents. I don't remember the exact line because I was busy elbowing him and telling him to stop ruining my life.

People thought he was my grandfather, and he was acting like it. I'm just trying to get through this without being completely humiliated and here was my father, dressed like a golfer, doing his best Jack Lemmon impression. His hypercongeniality annoyed the shit out of me.

I agreed to the tour as a goodwill gesture to Dad. It was dirt cheap, close to home, and a good school. If I wasn't going to VMI, the Colonel could settle on this.

I spoke to him in grunts for the rest of the day. I'd already decided that I was going to a small liberal arts school where there were no rednecks to be encountered on the way to the cafeteria. UVA looked like a big preppy acid trip, like a J. Crew catalog had exploded all over Thomas Jefferson's lawn. I'd grown up with Washington & Lee—once voted the most homophobic campus in the country—in my backyard. UVA seemed like a bigger version of W&L, with rows of fraternity houses and dormitories that looked like they'd been retrofitted by Howard Johnson. When we got to the oldest part of the campus, our bouncy guide got so worked up telling us about the honor of being allowed to live in one of the Jefferson-built pavilions which run alongside the central Lawn that she spat a foot in front of her.

I broke my silent treatment and whispered in Dad's ear, "Say it, don't spray it."

The Colonel pushed his glasses up his nose, crossed his arms, and gave me a stern look. "Pay attention," he said—naturally—loud enough for everyone to hear.

Miss Perky Tits continued, describing how fourth-year undergrads applied for these nineteenth-century rooms, which had neither showers nor bathrooms. At that moment, a young woman in a bathrobe walked toward the glorified outhouse, smiling and waving at the tour group. We all craned our necks to peer into the open room, where I noticed a small sink. I leaned into my father and said, "I'd *definitely* pee in the sink." He made a pained face. Terrorizing my father was so easy.

After the tour, I wandered into Plan 9 Records and bought two hard-to-find records: Fetchin' Bones' *Cabin Flounder* and Pylon's *Chomp*. This almost redeemed Charlottesville for me. Normally, by the time Dad and I were ready to leave a store or restaurant, he'd engaged the employees in conversations about their futures, offering to write them all job recommendations. Something clicked in the Colonel while we were in the record store—he recognized that this was my turf. He bought a Harry Connick Jr. cassette. I think he was, in his way, trying to bring us closer. Harry Connick Jr. was incorrect, but you gotta love him for trying.

The Yale tour guide wasn't nearly as cheerful as her UVA counterpart. I think her job was to scare off eighty percent of the kids who took the tour so that they wouldn't even bother applying. I went on this tour because a relative on my mother's side had gone here. Granted, he'd spent several years making bathtub gin before he eventually blew his brains out, but he was, nonetheless, a Yalie.

Mom and I dropped back about ten paces from the crowd, lingering in front of the theater where Jodie Foster had performed during her chubby period. I thought about John Hinckley stalking her and I burst into tears.

"It's so far away," I said.

"From home?" Mom asked.

"Yeah."

"From him?"

"Yeah."

It was the first time we'd spoken of Walker. She knew.

Mom was not a big toucher, but she put her hand on my neck and lightly scratched the back of my head. I got really sloppy, crying so hard I shook. Mom didn't know what to do, so she started crying too.

"Just to get here," I said, "we had to drive to the airport, then fly to New York, then take a train to New Haven—that's so far away. I feel like he won't be there when I get back. Like I got sent a hundred years into the future. I just want to go back. Can I call him?"

We found a pay phone and I sobbed into the phone.

"I'm not going to apply to Yale," I said to Walker. "I hate Yale."

"Is your mother there?" he asked.

"Yes, and she knows everything. It's fine."

"Hi, Walker," my mother yelled toward the phone.

Walker started laughing. We all did.

I handed the phone to Mom. I don't know why. It just seemed like the thing to do.

"I'm glad you're in the kid's life. You make him happy," she said, her voice cracking.

I yelled toward the phone "Happy, shit! He makes me miserable! Look at me. I'm a *mess*."

"But it's a good mess," Mom said. "Take care of each other," she added, handing the receiver back to me.

"I can't wait to see what you write about this one," Walker said. "Go have lunch with your mother. I love you."

"I love you too," I said.

It was such a relief to say that in front of my mother.

"Shhhhh!" Walker would say to stifle my grunts.

Walker was freaked out by the mere notion of having sex in my parents' house. I, on the other hand, got an illicit thrill from having *very quiet* orgasms ten feet above my sleeping parents. Walker was terrified that the Colonel might discover us, grow enraged, and report him to the police for sodomizing his seventeen-year-old son. Plus, being a well-mannered Southerner, he just thought it was inappropriate.

Mom knew all about our relationship and frequently counseled me when I came to her bawling about the hardships of a long-distance relationship. She often lamented that we couldn't be more open about our love. Her greatest concern was that dating a teacher meant that I had to hide in his closet. When I turned eighteen, she sent Walker a card that joked "He's finally legal!" Walker was completely horrified, but Mom's sense of humor often depended on someone else's horror.

When Walker came to visit, he was given my sister's bedroom. I'd always sneak him into my room after my parents had gone to bed. Mom knew we were having sex, but Dad was completely in the dark.

Since I'd spent the summer working in the theater in Richmond, my world was suddenly full of adult friends. We exchanged letters, talked on the phone, and visited one another. My parents encouraged me to spend more time with friends my age, concerned that I would miss out on seminal high school experiences like basketball games and parties. But I'd found my tribe and, after that, high school seemed more tedious than ever.

Lots of adults were encouraging my writing. As far as Dad was concerned, Walker was one of those people. Beyond that, we just didn't discuss it.

Mom, for some reason, relaxed the standard no-sex-in-the-house guideline for me. From the time I was born, Mom trusted that I had to learn from my own decisions. Her approach to parenting rarely encroached upon my freedom, especially when it came to Walker. She knew that our relationship posed huge challenges and she knew that our geographical separation was breaking our hearts. But over and over, she told me that she could tell I was in love.

"Are the greens greener?" she asked me.

I nodded yes.

"I ask all my children that same question when they say they're in love," she said. "You're the first one who knew what I was talking about."

She told me not to waste energy worrying. She told me to remember to enjoy every moment. She told me to stop obsessing over when I'd see him next. She told me to remember, above all, that we'd been blessed by love.

Dad, on the other hand, didn't even know that my relationship with Walker was romantic. To this day, I'm not sure *what* Dad knew about us. The Colonel and I silently agreed that we just wouldn't talk about that.

I do know that Dad absolutely adored Walker. They took long walks together and Walker cheerfully endured several of the Colonel's endless tours of the VMI campus. Sometimes, Mom and I would pack them off for a few hours to walk the dogs so the two of us could gossip in the kitchen. When Walker agreed with Dad that I should attend UVA, he scored *big* points. He quickly became a member of our family, which was healing for him, since he was estranged from his own family.

My siblings met and liked him, even the religious ones. As long as no one discussed the particulars of the relationship, they seemed okay with it. Some of them had been through messy divorces and some *really* messy marriages, so who were they to judge me? My sister Paige was very protective of me and called Walker on the phone every now and then to get to know him better. She too was taken in by his charm and social grace.

Even my brother Dwight liked him. Actually, that figures, since they were around the same age and both of them were Scorpios. The night the Gulf War broke out, in the spring of my senior year, Dwight took me to dinner. We hadn't spoken in several years because of his rift with Dad, but he wanted to make it clear to me that he accepted me as gay.

When I told Dwight about Walker, he asked me two hours' worth of questions that even Mom hadn't had the nerve to ask. He asked me the logistical details of our sex life, which I think is a perfectly reasonable thing for a straight person to ask. I mean, that's the Big Question, isn't it? If every straight person felt safe enough to ask a gay person how in the hell it works, homosexuality might not be so damn mystifying to them.

I told Dwight how hard it was to be separated from Walker. Lexington was over two hours away from Richmond, and when I started UVA that fall, we'd still be over an hour away from each other. Dwight took out a pen and drew a map of Virginia on the paper placemat. He traced a line between Charlottesville and Richmond, then drew a huge dot in the middle.

"Louisa County is halfway between Charlottesville and Richmond," he said, pointing to the line. "The two of you can get a house in Louisa and commute."

I stared at him, incredulous. My formerly homophobic brother was encouraging me to live with a man his own age.

"Real estate is dirt cheap there," he said, "and it would be a good investment for both of you."

"Are you *high?*" I asked him.

"You could get a dog," he said.

The waiter left another carafe of wine on our table and turned on the TV set. The United States was at war with Iraq. Peter Jennings announced that there had already been bombing and casualties. The screen was filled with images of flame and rubble. I worried that Dwight would have a Vietnam flashback right there in the restaurant.

"War is shit," he said loud enough for everyone to hear.

I went to the bathroom and when I came back, my brother was sobbing.

As I drove him home, three things were perfectly clear to me: we would never really win that war, someday Walker and I would have a dog, and I didn't know my brother at all.

the decline of western (virginia) civilization

Nothing brings people together like cheap draft beer. On occasion, I still went to a keg party during senior year, just to let myself be a high school student. I spent nearly every weekend in Richmond with Walker seeing plays, dance, and art. We had romantic three-hour dinners and all-night conversations. We were totally in love, even when we were fighting.

Going to a throw-down keg party was a welcome break from the very adult world I'd entered. This usually involved driving miles upon miles into the far reaches of Rockbridge County with friends whose idea of clear directions was "Um, yeah, I think there's a big oak tree where you're supposed to turn."

Once we arrived, typically I'd park in a field next to dozens of other cars. You'd think that people would have the sense to park in neat rows. But apparently this was half the fun. At the end of the party, when everyone was all good and wasted, drunks would rev their engines and get their wheels stuck in the mud. Trucks rolled into one another. Drunk boys cussed at other drunk boys. Insurance information was exchanged. Girls cried. Another Saturday night, down home.

Preston Watts's band the Safety Patrol was playing at one particular party that year. I was the lead singer in that band for three hours. I was ousted due to extensive creative differences. The song lyrics I proposed were not exactly what the other members had in mind. I was thinking Patti Smith, they were thinking Aerosmith. Plus, there was the whole "Kirk can't sing" factor. We parted amicably and they turned into a much more interesting band than I could ever have predicted.

When I got to the party, they were playing the Feelies' "Higher Ground," a pleasant soundtrack for my arrival. Not pleasant enough, mind you, for the drunk country boys to refrain from screaming for "Free Bird" at every available opportunity. But it was a good enough reason to stay.

Halfway through a cover of a Connells' song, Eddie McMullen and Jason Mathis started yahooing and stomping their cowboy-booted feet on the basement floor of whoever's house this was. Then they turned up a bottle of Jack Daniels and took turns swigging. To my shock, Eddie turned to me and handed me the bottle.

"Go for it, *Reeeeeeead,*" he said. I almost declined, then grabbed the bottle. This was an induction, I figured. They were accepting me as a redneck. After all, I had been born and raised in Rockbridge County just as they had. It made sense to get in touch with my roots, right?

I took a huge gulp of Jack Daniels and handed the bottle back to Eddie. After I swallowed, I let out a resounding "yahoo." It came out more slasher movie scream queen than drunk redneck hellraiser. But I was working on it.

"Whoo!" they screamed.

"Whoo!" I screamed along with them. "*Whoo!*"

Jason put his arm around me and walked me out of the basement. The three of us were headed toward the field, so car-cluttered it looked like a junkyard.

"I always park far away from everybody else," Eddie said.

"Whatcha drivin', Read?" Jason asked.

"Um, the baby-blue Honda Accord," I said, trying to make that sound as tough as I could.

These boys were the reason that hunting safety class was required in our school system. They wore blaze orange and listened to Merle Haggard. They got girls pregnant.

Eddie had a big truck, and he'd parked it on the other side of the field. I managed to step in two piles of cowshit en route, and my squeals made it obvious that I lived in town.

The bottle went around again, but this time no one hooted. Rather, they growled and slapped their hands on their jeans. I felt like I'd been thrown into one of those *National Geographic* spreads on lost aboriginal tribes.

Eddie got into the driver's seat, Jason jumped into the bed of the truck and I went around to the passenger side. Eddie wedged the bottle of Jack between the seats and motioned me toward the bed.

"We're goin' for a *riiiiiiide*," he said, grinning.

I thought this might be the part where they kill the fag.

I climbed up into the truck and Eddie took off.

"Hold on!" Jason said.

The truck went over huge potholes and ruts, throwing Jason and me two feet into the air. This was the most rural entertainment I'd ever had, unless one counted hayrides. But nobody counts hayrides. These guys were part of the group that called me *faggot* on the way to the cafeteria. I had zero-interest in this midnight joyride, except that maybe if they got to know me, they'd call me something else, like *buddy* or *guy*. I would have settled for *pardner*. This was a peace mission.

The whooping started again.

"Whoo!" screamed Eddie, revving his engine.

"Whoo!" replied Jason.

"Aaaahhhhh! Slow down!" I pleaded.

We went across a cattle guard, giving my butt another series of bruises. Eddie drove us several miles, sending the bottle back through the sliding window in the cab. Jason and I passed it back and forth. That very Friday at lunch time, I had volunteered to sell tee shirts for Students Against Drunk Driving. But that was only because it would look good for college.

Eddie pulled off to the side of the road and we jumped out. Jason and he were climbing a bank, so I followed them.

As we scaled the fence, it occurred to me to ask what we were doing.

"Cow-tipping," Eddie said. "Ever done it?"

"Um . . . *no*," I said. "What is that?"

"You go up to a cow who's asleep and you push it over," he explained.

Eddie and Jason had done this many times. I thought about turning back, telling them I'd wait in the truck, but I was curious. And as clichéd as it sounds, I wanted them to like me. That called for me to have a butch redneck moment, and I was rising to the challenge. I'd seen TV commercials against peer pressure to use alcohol and cigarettes. I'd never seen one about cow-tipping.

The guys found a cow. We crept up slowly. It was indeed asleep. Eddie and Jason lined up on the cow's left side. I guess that left me with the cow's butt. Jason and I looked at Eddie, who nodded his head. We all pushed hard against the cow, who, true to their word, tipped over.

The cow made a horrific noise, as if all the air was being pushed out of its lungs. I swear I felt the ground reverberate. I stood, staring at the fallen animal.

"Run, you stupid motherfucker!" Eddie screamed at me.

The field was pitch black. The stars were of no help. I heard the cow snorting and ran as fast as I could. I was sure that the cow and all of its progeny would trample me that night. I could barely see the fence. I ran smack into it, then grabbed the post and flipped over the fence.

Jason and Eddie were laughing, slapping each other's hands. They were patting each other way too hard on the back, the way men do when they want to be intimate.

As we returned to the party, I rode shotgun. My rear end had simply been through enough. As much as I wanted to be like these boys, I just didn't have it in me. I was ready to puke from the whiskey, though I'd consumed only a fraction of their take. And I don't think one's supposed to feel guilty after cow-tipping. I was a pathetic excuse for a redneck.

But it worked. When I saw those guys in the hall from that point on, they gave me a friendly punch on the arm.

"Whoo!" they'd scream.

"Whoo!" I'd reply.

"Whoo!" we'd scream together.

hands

The winter of my senior year, Walker and I went to hear Allen Ginsberg read at VMI. Gordon Ball, a Ginsberg scholar, was on the faculty of the school, which explained the two-night stint at J. M. Hall. Both colleges had a habit of employing liberal arts professors who were actually liberal, despite the neo-conservative bent of both schools.

"This is *weird*," Walker and I repeated to each other like a mantra.

J. M. Hall is often used for weddings, which escapes logic. Behind the stage, there's a massive mural depicting the Battle of New Market, in which many VMI-trained soldiers were killed. The mural is filled with smoke, soldiers charging, and soon-to-be-bloody bayonets.

The entire cadet corps, 1,000 strong, filled the seats. The rest of us were cultured or just plain curious townies, as yet unsure what in the world Allen Ginsberg was doing here.

Sally Mann walked by us, gesturing to the mural. "It's *ghastly*," she said to no one in particular. I'd been to her house on a field trip in fourth grade. Preston and I were sent outside for giggling when we saw some of her nudes and couldn't contain ourselves. She'd photographed many of my friends in a book that would later be denounced by right-wingers as child pornography. My favorite was one of a twelve-year-old girl laying on the hood of a filthy car. The word *DOOM* was fingered into the grime.

Ginsberg appeared from the back of the stage. He was carrying all sorts of drums and a squeezebox. He opened with a dirge, playing an instrument I'd never seen and repeating lines ten and fifteen times.

He read *Howl* in its entirety, which was breathtaking. All the writers I'd ever heard read from their work were hideously boring, holding up their newly published books and flipping through pages as if some spirit would tell them which was the correct poem to read next. The worst was when they took copious sips of water, as if that twenty-line poem had completely taxed their voice. Allen Ginsberg didn't take a single swig. Child was hydrated.

Toward the end of the hour, he read a haiku.

Two middle-aged men
Lying in bed together
Hold hands

The cadets moaned audibly in disapproval. I reached over and squeezed Walker's hand, then realized that we couldn't hold hands there. The cadets had managed to maintain polite silence throughout *Howl* and even poems that mentioned boy-love and Vaseline. But that one really scared the shit out of them. It remains the most beautiful combination of words I've ever heard.

After the last poem, the liberal townies stood and cheered. The cadets, for the most part, remained seated and waited until they were allowed to file back to barracks.

"What a waste," I said to Walker, looking askance at all the crewcuts bobbing above white uniforms.

"It's perfect," he responded. "This night was perfect."

That night Walker stayed at a thirty-dollar motel on the edge of Lexington. He refused to stay at my house because he'd just been there and didn't want the Colonel to get suspicious. I knew I couldn't sleep over with him, but stayed long enough to make love and read him nearly two hours' worth of my journal. During one of the poems, I banged on the headboard in lieu of a drum. We laughed so hard the people in the next room kicked the wall.

The next night, I returned to J. M. Hall alone. Ginsberg performed for another blistering hour and a half, reading "Kaddish" and a piece that repeated the line "Don't smoke." That one actually made the cadets laugh. Somehow, he'd won them back. The room got warmer and everyone seemed to be breathing. It felt safe again.

Afterward, I wanted to shake his hand, maybe get a book signed. He was mobbed by fans who seemed to be doing all the talking. I never understood why people shouldered each other for face-time with their icons, only to blab their inane life stories. Why would he care?

I sat cross-legged on the front pew, about twenty feet away. It was close enough, I'd decided. When the crowd eased, he looked over at me. I was writing a poem in my notebook when I caught his glance. He shot me his best dirty-old-man smile and I nervously put my pen in my teeth. I don't know why. Then Allen Ginsberg winked at me. A hippie woman with a messy French braid pushed her way in front of him, ranting loudly about Vietnamese children. Sufficiently blessed, I walked home.

backstage

On the way to Richmond, Valerie wouldn't stop kicking the dashboard. She was chain-smoking, squealing with excitement about the concert. Shelley was in the backseat, probably rolling her eyes at Valerie.

We picked up Walker, and Shelley and he shared the backseat and talked quietly. I was nervous about what they'd think of each other.

The Indigo Girls were amazing. I'd never sensed so much estrogen in one place. Grown women were jumping up and down, screeching. It was like Beatlemania, but in Birkenstocks.

Walker knew the old theater well, so towards the end, he showed us a doorway that led to a tunnel that ran under the stage. "Want to go backstage?" he asked.

We followed him through the passageway. We felt the vibrations of thousands of dancing feet above us. We turned a corner, ascended a staircase, and—BAM—we were backstage.

We stood in the wing, watching as they wrapped up their set. A hefty woman with horn-rimmed glasses approached us, barking.

"What are these people doing back here?" she yelled at several of her minions.

Just before she could get her hands on us, we ran back through the tunnel, whooping. A minute later, we returned. The Indigo

Girls were standing backstage. Valerie ruined our undetected views by screaming "Amy!"

The amply sized woman wheeled back around, stomping toward us.

Walker led us out the stage door. The Indigo Girls had jumped into a tiny red car and were speeding away. Valerie sprinted after them, smacking one of the windows with all her might. Shelley, Walker, and I stared as Valerie practically threw herself in front of the car, which was doing forty in an alley. I figured it must be a lesbian thing.

It started drizzling, then pouring. Walker took the keys and said the girls and I should stay dry under the theater's marquee and that he'd bring the car around. Once Walker was out of earshot, Shelley turned to me and said, "He's the sweetest person I've ever met. If you don't marry him, I'll kick your butt."

It was exactly what I needed to hear.

The one person I never formally came out to was Shelley. Why hadn't I afforded her the courtesy of a trip to the river? I owed her that. It wasn't that she was Mormon. We'd drifted apart in the way that best friends do. She'd disappeared into daily practices for basketball and volleyball. I'd disappeared into a flurry of social and extracurricular chaos.

She already knew in many respects. I'd told her about my friendship with Rich, leaving out the sex part. We'd shared a mutual obsession with Mr. Leland, though we'd never discussed it as a traditional crush.

Shelley suffered the greatest indignity a former best friend can sustain. She heard it from my lips during twelfth-grade English class. We were giving oral presentations on our senior thesis projects. Mine was a paper on the way Tennessee Williams buried homosexuality in his plays.

"I'm interested in how Tennessee Williams treats homosexuality because I'm gay and I want to write about that."

I mean, everyone already knew, or so I thought. And it wasn't a big deal, or so I thought. For Shelley, that day was mortifying. She'd seen my play, she'd read my poems, she'd heard it from other people. But I'd never told her directly.

One night toward the end of our senior year, Shelley and I sat down on a stone wall outside a party at a friend's house. We didn't talk much anymore. Our lives were so different at that point.

"Why didn't you tell me?" she asked

"I don't know."

"Hearing about it in class, in front of everyone else, I wanted to die."

"I'm sorry," I said.

"You told other people."

"I know. I'm sorry."

"Did you think I wouldn't understand?" she asked.

"I don't know."

"How could you think that?"

"I'm sorry," I said. "This has been really hard."

"I could have helped you."

She didn't say anything else. A moment passed. I took a long sip of beer then handed the can to her.

"We have to stay in better touch," I said. The suggestion was well-intentioned, but it was the hollow thing people say to each other when a friendship has run its course.

"I know," she said.

We were both headed to college in a matter of months. We looked at one another with weary eyes, wondering how we could recreate that magical freshman year when we'd been bookends.

"There's a concert tonight," she said, turning her gaze to the stars.

The sky was full of lonely constellations. We both lay on our backs in the grass. Our hands found each other and we locked our sweaty fingers together.

We'd always tried to see the same shooting star, but usually we caught them one at a time. That night, with two years of silence between us, we stared at the same set of stars. Out of the corner of my eye I looked at her to make sure she wasn't crying. Just to her left, a star fell.

"See that?" I said.

"Yeah," she said. "Finally."

blood

Ronnie Coleman wrote a term paper on AIDS in 1986, the year Ronald Reagan first said the word in public.
This was also around the time I started having sex with Rich. When he pulled a box of condoms from his drawer, I had a vague idea of why we needed them. But I still wanted to proceed without them. He insisted that we always use them.

I read Ronnie's term paper and it scared the hell out of me. As I read it, I heard a deep demonic narration in my head. "This is what you get," I heard again and again, "because you're a *faggot*."

AIDS was too sciencey for me. My eighth-grade term paper was on censorship, Tipper Gore's assault on free speech in the music industry, and the Dead Kennedys. The band had released *Frankenchrist* the previous year with a poster inside by H. R. Giger called *Landscape XX "Where are we coming from?"*, which had a repeating pattern of erect penises. Fans nicknamed it *Penis Landscape*. The album was seized by San Francisco police which resulted in a nasty court battle.

I called Jello Biafra, the Dead Kennedys lead, and actually talked to him. He humored me because his lawyer and he were amused that a thirteen-year-old was writing about their case. When I got him on the phone, I was so nervous that I asked utterly inane, dorky questions.

I was one of those small-town skateboard punks who carried

a skateboard but couldn't go very fast, let alone attempt a ramp. In less polite terminology, I was a poseur. I needed Jello Biafra's smart social critiques every bit as much as I needed Suicidal Tendencies' rage sputtering tunes like "I Shot Reagan." I used to scream that one at my parents, both of whom were Republicans.

"*I shot Reagan! And I'll shoot him again and again and again!*"

"Don't talk like that!" my father would yell.

"It's a *song*," I'd counter, then continue my screaming.

Reagan's failure to act sooner on AIDS cost hundreds of thousands of lives. The media ignored AIDS until Rock Hudson died. I easily could have been infected at age fourteen. Prevention messages didn't even reach our school until 1988, when I was in ninth grade. A social worker from the public health department came into our classroom with a white coat and wrote the word *ABSTINENCE* on the blackboard in capital letters. She underlined it twice, then told us how birth control pills didn't protect girls from HIV. She said absolutely nothing that would be relevant to a young gay man. Everything was framed in terms of boy/girl sex, so in a perverse way, I felt protected from the very thing that was decimating gay men. At that point, I was already sexually active with an older man. Had that man been infected, he could have passed it onto me without even knowing. People just weren't getting tested much at that point, especially in small towns.

Walker and I were together for nine months before we got tested my senior year. We'd had sex dozens of times, always protected—except for once. It was New Year's Eve and we were in New York City. Being in love made condoms a horrible fact of life. We both hated them.

But Walker had quite a past, and he'd never been tested. Our lapse in safety made it all the more urgent for us to get tested. It wasn't just about him anymore. It was about my health and our health as well.

I called the Lexington heath department and asked about HIV testing. Richmond had far more testing sites, but Walker was so resistant to the idea of being tested at all that I had to ambush him. He'd arrived in Lexington by Greyhound the first Friday in January and I knew that he wouldn't put up a fight about it in my parents' home.

We'd been up all night talking about it. We'd exchanged ten-page letters about it. He'd been putting off the test for years because he was too scared to know. During our nine months as a couple, he'd kept saying that he couldn't deal with the results if he were HIV-positive. He said we should wait a month until this or that job deadline had passed. It took two and a half weeks to get results back, so getting tested was basically a commitment to live in terror. We'd run through a series of "what-if" scenarios as if we were making a grocery list. What if only he was infected? What if he'd infected me? What if he was sick? How would we tell my parents? How would we continue our relationship? Would I have to drop out of high school? Would we get those purple spots?

In February, we drove to the health department. It was bitter cold, and Walker was, as usual, underdressed. For some reason, he'd left his coat in Richmond, so I bundled him up in my mother's coat. He looked hilarious, which was a nice distraction—for me, anyway. As we ascended the steps to the health department, I kept calling him by my mother's name—"Come on, Suzanne."

The receptionist had us fill out forms and told us we would be tested separately. We agreed that I would go first. He sat out in the hall, reading old *Highlights for Children* magazines, which was the extent of the waiting room literature. Well, there was also a wall of pamphlets on herpes, syphilis, and other creepy crawlies, but Walker wasn't exactly knocking over furniture to get to them.

The nurse was very gentle with me. She asked me questions about my entire sexual history. How many times I'd had sex with Rich, who'd done what and whether we'd used condoms. I didn't tell her about New Year's Eve with Walker, because I knew it had been a mistake. I didn't need her confirmation. I had to give her approximations of how many times I'd had sex with Rich and Walker, which freaked me out. The numbers seemed so gigantic. I *had* to be sick. Then she drew my sex life on a clipboard in a flowchart made of the kind of bubbles that usually contain dialogue in comic strips.

She asked me if the man in the lobby was my *partner*. I said yes, even though I hated that word. *Partner* was someone with whom one had a business. I liked *boyfriend,* but Walker said it felt weird to him because he was no longer a boy. Walker liked *lover.* I told him that that word made me feel like a dowdy French woman who serviced married men in a rat-infested apartment. So we each used our own words.

She tied off my arm and drew my blood, then gave me a phone number to call in fifteen days. She handed me condoms in a brown paper bag, the same sort of bag in which Mom packed my school lunches. I always made Walker get condoms. I didn't know if there was an age limit for condoms, and I would never risk getting stopped at checkout for underage condom purchasing. Who needs that humiliation?

When Walker visited, I'd steal condoms from my parents, one at a time so they wouldn't notice. I didn't have lube, so we'd use the lotions from hotels, most of which surely contained ingredients that weren't compatible with latex condoms. Who knew?

I'd never seen so many condoms. There were mint ones for oral sex, which we later discarded because they were revolting. There were ribbed ones and multicolored ones, which made us laugh. Once, my father had gotten a black condom from a dispenser in a gas station bathroom. When my mother saw it, she started laughing, which I'm sure didn't help the Colonel's erection.

"You're next," I told Walker, fully aware that his sexual history would take a lot more than ten minutes to recount. His file would be a lot fatter than mine by the time we left.

He'd lived in New York before moving to Richmond. He told me stories about having sex on subway cars. He told me stories about passing out from MDA and ludes other drugs I'd never even heard of. He told me stories about a dazzling procession of men tucked so far back in his history that even *I* couldn't be jealous. I savored each story as if it was another facet of him I was getting to know. New lovers collect sexual anecdotes for insight into their new mates and for ammunition and leverage in fights to come.

In the lobby, I'd started writing my will and was on the third page when Walker emerged twenty-five minutes later. He carried a similar brown bag and covered his face.

"What took ya so long?" I asked. We laughed, then stopped, because we knew that both of us were dying.

When we got home, we tried to have sex, but we were both so scared that we just ended up holding each other. I told him I would take care of him when he got sick. He said he deserved to die because he'd infected me and knew I'd die before I got out of my teens.

When we parted at the end of the weekend, it was characteristically dramatic. Our entire relationship was cinematic, at least to us. It was sort of Merchant-Ivory because it was so grand and gut-wrenching. But it was also sort of *I Love Lucy* because we were both dilemma-prone. Sobbing, dying, bidding farewell for possibly the last time, Walker boarded the Greyhound and I went home to continue work on my will.

For the next two weeks, we wrote each other daily letters expressing his guilt, my forgiveness, our undying love, and my sudden honesty that I would be really pissed at him if he infected me just because he was a drug-taking slut who sat on strangers and woke up in unidentified apartments. How could he live like that? I couldn't live like that. I wanted love and marriage and a house and dogs. Maybe this *was* a punishment from God. Maybe my born-again brother was right.

I'd continued writing my will, the pages of which numbered in the double digits. I didn't even have very much stuff to bequeath. I made a mix tape each day of that waiting period, full of melancholy songs by Bob Marley, U2, Tracy Chapman, and Chicago. *Chicago.* I didn't tell any of my friends or my parents what was happening. I couldn't focus at school and stayed home sick three days in a row.

On Valentine's Day, we both called in for our results. I went first, because Walker knew that if I were positive, he was too. Plus, he just plain didn't want to know. I called the health department and gave the woman my ID number. I'd been calling five days in a row, hoping that my results would arrive early. They could only give results over the phone if one were negative. Otherwise, one had to get test results in person, according to state law. But if they said that I had to come in, didn't I already know?

She told me I was negative. I thanked her. Then I realized that Walker could still be positive, so I asked him to call. He was negative, too. I wrote squishy thank-you notes to the nurse who drew my blood and to the receptionist. It's just how my mother raised me.

Then I told Mom. The conversation was quick, one of those I-just-want-you-to-know exchanges. I just want you to know I took the trash out. I just want you to know I dented the fender. I just want you to know I flunked a test and need your signature.

"I just want you to know I got tested for AIDS and I don't have it."

Mom's eyes opened wide. "When did you do that?"

"Two weeks ago. I just found out. Walker's okay, too."

"Have you been worrying all this time?" she asked.

"I didn't want you to think about it."

"I would have worried with you. That's what mothers do."

"Thanks." I didn't want to tell my mother I was getting an HIV test until I had the happy ending in hand. Suspense is only fun if it lasts ninety minutes and involves popcorn.

"Don't get sick," she said. "Please don't get sick."

"I won't. I promise."

We never told Dad and I didn't tell any of my friends.

Every April, like government-sanctioned vampires, the Red Cross came to get the blood of us high schoolers. They'd pull up a trailer out front of LHS and for days we'd hear loudspeaker propaganda about blood donation as the benchmark of responsible citizenship. The athletic teams banded together and competed with each other to see who could give the most pints.

At lunch, I looked at my half-pint of chocolate milk. They're going to take *two* of these? I wasn't convinced that good citizenship was worth that much blood.

For years, my mother had made sandwiches for the participants in the annual blood drive at VMI. I'd gone with her many times, helping make sandwiches and watching as the cadets stretched out on lawn chairs. They got orange juice and half a peanut butter-and-jelly sandwich after their donation. Some of them got dizzy. A few of them fainted. These men, who at eighteen seemed older than I'd ever get, toppled into the arms of townie women in their fifties.

I thought giving blood might give Mom one of those maternal tingles of pride. I finally gave in to the relentless serve-your-country messages pouring out of the speakers during morning and afternoon announcements. I told Mom I was going to give blood at school. I could see her fathom the legacy of it all.

"Do they make sandwiches?" she asked.

The best perk, of course, was that blood donors got to miss half a period to give blood and recover. I chose to donate during trigonometry, a species of math so diabolical that I was struggling to get a low-B. Senior year, everyone relaxes about grades, but a C might impact my college admission. I dreaded the arrival of a letter from UVA's admissions office, reading "You're *un*invited."

I stood in line outside the trailer. The girl in front of me had, without much exaggeration, been through a third of the starting lineup of any given LHS athletic team one could name. That was the operative school legend, anyhow. The nurses knew her by name and closed the door to the trailer.

The girl emerged ten minutes later with a bandage on her arm. She'd done her good deed.

I took a deep breath. The last time I'd had a needle in my arm was during my HIV test. I was so relieved that this was a gift, not a test. People always appreciate gifts, don't they?

The nurse handed me a form to complete which asked me questions about my sex life since 1977. I was precocious, but not *that* precocious. The questions weren't just about who one had had sex with. They were about being a man and having sex with other men. The form wasn't specific about what sex meant, just if one had had it. And I had. I considered lying, but wanted to ask the nurse what it meant. I handed her back the clipboard.

"I'm HIV-negative," I said. "I got tested two months ago."

She looked out the window of the trailer to make sure no one was on the steps.

"Have you had sex with another man since 1977?" she asked, fixing her eyes on the clipboard.

"Yes, but I'm *negative.*"

"I'm sorry, hon. You're not eligible."

"But some of the people who've come in here are not using condoms. They're more of a risk than I am. I have a boyfriend. Just one boyfriend."

"I'm sorry. That's our policy."

"It's a stupid policy," I said.

"It's to keep contaminated blood out of the general population," she said.

What the hell is the general population? Whatever it was, I guess I wasn't in it. Contaminated. I was *contaminated.*

I went back to trigonometry, furious that my charity had been refused, but even angrier because my original plan, getting the hell out of class, had been dashed.

That afternoon, I heard the principal's voice come over the loudspeaker to thank all of the brave and generous students who'd given their blood. She quoted a statistic about how desperately the Red Cross needed blood.

enchantment

Walker was neither willing nor allowed to attend my senior prom in 1991. He looked great in a tux, granted, but the image of us slow dancing to a Holiday Inn cover band *was* a little creepy. He sent me a photo from his senior prom, which was right out of the bland mid-sixties, before people started to Go Ask Alice.

I'd decided to be vampy that year. I'd played it relatively safe the previous year, with white tie and tails. I'd worn Converse high tops, which I'd splattered with fabric paint, and ripped jeans. My junior prom date, Johnna Griffith, had expected something far more audacious out of me.

We'd known each other since we were four. Soon after we'd met, I'd told her mother I wanted to take Johnna to the VMI post exchange for ice cream, to which she said I'd have to save up my money. I returned to show her a handful of change. Reluctantly, Mrs. Griffith let her little girl go on her first date. To this day, she calls me her "future son-in-law." Mrs. Griffith knows I'm gay, because when I wrote my coming-out play, she called the editor of our local paper and pitched the story. Johnna will likely be a senator or judge or something that will require her to carefully bury her association with the likes of me.

For our senior prom, the theme was "Sea of Enchantment." Surely, a copy of *Back to the Future* had gotten stuck in someone's

VCR. I'd considered going as an octopus, then relented. I had a wooden lizard head bolo tie that was garish enough. Walker sent a killer jacket with tails and a pair of black cowboy boots. The out-fit's final touch was a pair of ripped jeans. And not just knee rips, but crotch and butt rips as well. It would be my little farewell to LHS.

Samantha, my senior prom date, had played Sleeping Beauty to my Prince Charming in a community theater production our freshman year. I kissed her onstage and got to wear tights and a ridiculous green crushed velvet outfit. We had a duet, "Where or When," and I sang so badly that the music director had to rearrange it twice. I mean, it wasn't all *that* horrible. Kids singing is cute. Kids singing badly is still cute. Samantha fared better, since she was the school's reigning theater bitch. She had that long drama hair and when she was in the room, you always knew it.

She was delighted to have a non-romantic date. I mean, why foul up prom with all the insanity of a real boy? Our friends had a big group dinner, then Samantha and I raced to my house be-fore hitting prom. I'd gotten a wicked sunburn earlier that day on our senior trip to Lake Shenandoah. Samantha rubbed Noxema into my shoulders, which were throbbing red. Romantic.

When we got up to the reception table, Odessa Meyers, who was acting as a chaperone, took one look at my jeans and said, "No, uh-uh. That's against the rules. And it's *tacky*. I can't be-*lieve* you're *wearing* those rags."

I just looked at Samantha and smirked, the consummate smart-ass. We went home and I changed into a pair of unripped jeans.

After I'd wanted so badly to stir up the school with a gay date my junior year, I was especially furious that no one seemed to care anymore that I was gay. They just didn't want me to wear ripped jeans.

I got completely shitfaced at the after-party. I decided it was a perfect time to tell my friend Bobby how I really felt about him, so I pulled him into the bushes. We started talking and I cut right to it.

"I've always had feelings for you," I said. Bobby, bless him, just sat there. Shortly thereafter, I started throwing up. He put his hands on my shoulders as I puked. It was not one of my most dignified moments.

I'd embarrassed myself on numerous occasions with Bobby. Having a crush on someone who is hopelessly straight is an ugly rite of passage for nearly every queer teenager. When we were best friends our junior year, I used to read poems to him. Bobby couldn't have been less interested in these recitations, since he was the ultimate guy's guy. But he always listened. He'd even let me hug him goodnight. Either he was being extremely charitable or utterly clueless. With straight boys, that's a fine line.

Samantha appeared at the top of the yard. "Prom date? Are you throwing up? *Poor* prom date!"

Bobby sat back and we looked at each other. We said nothing.

His girlfriend Kate walked up to the edge of the bushes. "Robert," she said. "Can we go for a walk? I want to have a philosophical conversation."

She was one of my best friends, but I wanted to snap her little neck. Bobby and she were *always* having philosophical conversations. I couldn't even get the child to count to ten. What was her secret? I mean, besides being a girl?

Samantha and three other friends carried me through the back gate of my yard. My parents were out of town and our family friend Vera was staying with me and the dogs. When she heard us outside, Vera had gone for her gun, which she kept by her pillow.

We were boisterous, and I was stumbling all over the patio, knocking over flower pots.

Vera opened the French doors in the back of the house.

"Honey, what in the world is you doin'?" she asked.

"One too many," Samantha said, pointing out the TV movie of the week that was unfolding before us.

"Y'all take him upstairs," Vera said. "I'm gonna bring you some aspirin, baby."

When Vera got to my bedside, I was close to passed-out.

"I told him," I said.

"You told him what, darlin'."

"That I was in love with him once."

"Well, hell," she said. "That's a good reason as any to get all tore up."

My senior year, I decided to pay a visit to the therapist who saw almost all of my brother's entire family. My brother was receiving enormous amounts of attention for his mental health peccadilloes, and I wanted a piece of that action.

"I want to understand my brother," I told the therapist, when he asked why I was seeing him.

I made sure he was taking notes, then proceeded to reel off a dazzling litany of my family's dysfunction. I couldn't have fictionalized anything this useful. If you're a writer and you can survive the slings and arrows of blood relatives, you'll never go hungry for material. My mother told me that as a child, I'd threaten siblings by storming upstairs screaming, "Wait until the book comes out."

I told him about my parents being eighteen years apart in age. I told him about my relentless infatuations with older men. He calmly listened. To my horror, he stopped taking notes. I wanted him to take notes, goddamn it. How was I supposed to be a freak case study requiring intensive supervision if he wasn't even taking notes? Surely, I thought, this therapist could see that I was the poster child for pyschopharmacology.

I went through generations and generations of my relations, listing some of their particular maladies: media spectacles, public humiliation, physical abuse, suicide, alcohol and drug addiction, spousal battery, wrecked cars, suicide, police records, et cetera. I repeated the words *et cetera* three times and he stopped me.

"What about *you?*" he asked.

"What *about* me?" I said, a little combatively.

"You're the most normal one," he said. "You're fine. You don't need to be here. I don't think you need to come back."

Why wasn't he cooperating? Why wasn't he prescribing me meds or shipping me off to a celebrity psychiatric treatment facility in sunny Southern California? Just as the school board had short-circuited my master plan for a media circus, this man was telling me I was okay. This was really screwing up my commitment to teenage angst.

In a panic, I started spewing an incoherent oral book report on Walker Percy's *Lancelot.* I told the good doctor how I really related to the guy who could only see bits of signs from his nuthouse window. I'd made a tee shirt out of the only letters the character could see: FREE & MA B. He still wasn't taking notes.

"You're smart," he said, halfway through the session. "Go."

"Well, then, doc, tell me something. Why am I attracted to older men?"

"You just *are,*" he said. "Some things you just can't figure. Bob Dylan said that."

"Some things you just can't figure?"

In college, I went to the counseling center for eight free sessions. After that, they scheduled additional appointments only if they thought it would be in society's best interest. After fifty-four sessions, my counselor had used me as a case study in her dissertation. I was audiotaped and videotaped and discussed at staff meetings. The whole thing was thrilling. Maybe I really *was* disturbed.

I later saw a lesbian therapist who'd legally changed her name to Joy. She said that being on the cusp of Capricorn and Aquarius was the reason I was both "anal retentive and all over the place at the same time."

In the end, my first therapist was right. Some things you just can't figure.

indestructible

When my mother had a heart attack in April of my senior year, she drove herself to the hospital. That was classic Suzanne behavior. The emergency room intake worker asked her to have a seat. Mom was admitted and diagnosed with angina.

That night, I found Dad sitting in their bedroom, facing the wall. The Colonel was crying so hard he couldn't sit up straight, and I sat on the floor and held both of his hands. The only words I could make out were "she's my heart."

Our family physician Dr. Mundy saw a lot of us that week. I went in a few days later for my college physical. He always dictated details of my life into a tape recorder, such as how I was doing in Latin or what I wanted to be when I grew up. That day, he said I appeared concerned about my mother. He turned the tape recorder off and said, "It's not your mother I'm worried about. She'll live to be a hundred. I'm worried about your father."

It never occurred to me to worry about Dad. He was seventy-one and still ran three miles every other day. He didn't smoke and hadn't had any significant medical problems, apart from prostate surgery ten years prior. (To his horror, Mom had told everyone at the time that he was having a "male D&C." It was the first time I ever saw the Colonel hooked up to machines. He had a catheter, so when Mom and I walked into the hospital room, he screamed, "Stop walking! You're jiggling my tee tee!")

About a week after her heart attack, Mom had an angioplasty. She had to quit smoking and eat better, but other than that, the doctor described her as "indestructible." She hassled the doctor to let her go home early because she missed our dogs.

"Don't you miss us?" I asked her.

"Mostly the dogs," Mom joked.

Two of my siblings were getting divorces that week, Mom was in the hospital, and Dad was being a drill sergeant. When I wasn't at the hospital, I hid in my room, writing.

I was finishing the last few scenes in a new play and Douglas had encouraged me to write something dramatic in the second act. The play was closely modeled on my family, and the places I'd had the most trouble were the spots where the narrative diverged from reality.

I went into one of those strange writer trances and wrote a long scene for the top of act two. All twelve characters are on stage and the father slugs his drunk son, who falls headfirst into a fishpond. Immediately following the punch, the father has a stroke and collapses.

The following evening, my real life father had a stroke.

I was taking a phone message when Mom ran into the house and asked for help. Dad had lost feeling in his left side and was fighting the idea of going to the hospital. He tried to get out of the car but couldn't. I convinced him to sit back down in the car but he wanted to lay down in bed. I told him he'd either go peacefully with me or we'd call the ambulance.

I pulled the car around the loop at the entrance to the ER. The admissions lady was on the phone. My father was dying so I screamed at her and banged on the window. I told her to get her ass outside and tend to my father. She just looked at me. Hospital personnel must *love* concerned relatives.

He was near death when we arrived. The doctor said, "Fifteen minutes more. That's it."

Once he was in intensive care, he squeezed my hand and started spitting out a stream of aphorisms: Don't give up on Christ, Watch your diet, Don't let people make you drink, Take care of your mother, Don't let her lift heavy things.

When I gave him water and asked him to calm down, he got furious.

"I want out of here *right now*. I can't move. Dr. Mundy said I could leave tonight."

He made up the part about leaving. He asked us for periodic reports on his blood pressure and sometimes I deflated the numbers to make him feel better.

"I have eyes. I can see that machine. I can count. Didn't they teach you to count? Shakespeare didn't use vulgar language. It bothers your mother and you don't need that crap. I don't want to get out of shape. I'm training for the cancer race—5K. Can't run 10K anymore. Got the garden in—tomatoes, everything."

I just kept squeezing his hand. Other family members filed into the room to sit with him. One by one, he gave us the apocalyptic advice of a dying man. He mistook my nephew for me, so he got a double dose.

Mom sat down on the edge of the bed. Dad kept channeling Moses, scaring the hell out of his children. Mom clapped her hands in his face and said, "Touch your nose."

Dad tried, but ended up poking his chin.

"Where's your belly button?" Mom said.

The Colonel pointed to his neck and finally cracked a smile. "Jerks," he said to all of us.

It seemed like we hadn't laughed in weeks.

I hadn't finished my final English paper on time, as usual. My problem with deadlines started in preschool and had gotten progressively worse. Our class hadn't written a formal paper like this in months. Mrs. Mutispaugh was always sending us outside to do group work. If we read *Macbeth*, we'd have bloody swordfights and freaky renditions of the witch scenes.

We'd made home movies and collaborated on group poems, but we'd never written a paper with footnotes in that class. Mrs. Mutispaugh was interested in how literature was seeping into our bones, how we were integrating it into our lives, how it was exploding inside us. The joke among her students was that the fastest way to an A was to spill your guts and make it read like poetry.

We'd been reading Camus and Sartre. We were at the end of the last semester of high school, when all that bleak existentialism looks pretty damn accurate. It's risky, actually, letting loose *The Myth of Sisyphus* on a bunch of eighteen-year-olds who have at one point or another considered suicide.

I was banking on the fact that enough people would read their papers aloud that I could slip out unnoticed. I'd been up late every night that week talking on the phone with Walker. Dad had left a note on the staircase, stapled to the phone bill. It was addressed to Mom and me, and it referred to the length of our phone calls as "extravagant and insulting." Though Mom and Dad had both recovered in a matter of weeks, Dad was still a little punchy from the steroids he'd been prescribed. Mom promised she'd intercept the next phone bill.

Several students read their papers, which mostly bandied about big words such as *nothingness* and *nihilism*. Listening to these junior philosophers was making my skin crawl. Those Frenchies were so *depressing*. I was up for a happy, *funny* paper on existentialism. Something peppy. Something with a beat to it. I mean, thank God we didn't have to do term papers on Charles Dickens, but *still*.

Preston raised his hand. He was a surefire candidate to have a perverse take on all this sad shooting-an-Arab-on-the-beach poo poo. At boys' slumber parties in fourth grade, Preston told all of us where babies come from. He told the nastiest jokes we'd ever heard. He even had books about sex because he had liberal parents. With Preston, you could always bet that he was going to say something about sex. And after all this morbid drivel, I was ready for his treatise on sexistentialism.

The assignment to consider was "what is the Authentic Man?" Preston went to the podium, cleared his throat, and began.

"Kirk Read is the Authentic Man," he said.

All the breath rushed out of me. I sank back into my desk and put my hands flat so no one could see how much I was shaking.

Preston went on for three pages about how I'd been true to myself at great personal risk. He called me brave for coming out and said he'd learned a new definition of honesty by watching me live. He told a story about how, in eighth grade, I kicked a boy out of a slumber party for using the word *faggot*. He said he knew several kids in school who hadn't come out yet but told Preston I made them feel safer. A lot of what he said was news to my classmates. They knew I was gay, but I doubt they'd ever thought about the shit you take when you're out in high school. As he spoke, I kept thinking *I got away with it*.

He finished, looking directly at me and swinging the final stapled page back to its place. Then people started clapping. I don't know who started, and I don't remember how long it went on. My eardrums were rattling, like I was in an airplane about to touch ground.

I couldn't look up. While they were clapping, my mind raced through every indignity I'd ever sustained at that fucking school, sometimes from people who were now clapping. Every shove, every epithet, every time I was too scared to walk down a certain hallway. Every time I got threatened. Every time I didn't report it. Every time I got called *sissy* or *faggot* or *homo*. Every time I sat in class waiting for a teacher to mention gay people. Every time they didn't. Every long walk to the cafeteria. Every time I stopped breathing in the locker room while I stripped to my underwear. Every time I saw a girl wearing her boyfriend's class ring, knowing Walker could go to jail because of me. Every time I burped up acid because my stomach was churning so hard. Every second I spent assessing how I dressed, how I walked, whether I lisped. Every hour I spent writing the things I couldn't say out loud. Every time I shared those words with other people.

home

The word at graduation rehearsal was that we were going to press condoms into Principal Terry's hand during our congratulatory handshakes. I thought it was a marvelous idea and was elated that someone else in my class had been evil enough to think of it.

We were lined up in the long hallway at the cavernous VMI basketball stadium, boys in red and girls in white. By that point, the prank had been downgraded from condoms to Starlight Mints. Peppermints were perfect, someone had reasoned, because red and white are the school colors. I took two, figuring I'd steady my dirty little tongue with one during the valedictory speeches, which I feared would be peppered with Simon and Garfunkel lyrics.

When the announcement of graduates' names began, I heard whoops for every third graduate, which seemed inappropriate given the occasion, but touching nonetheless. I secretly hoped that someone would offer up a big final whoop for the faggot.

At Mrs. Terry's side, there was a small pile of mints.

She announced, "Meade Kirkpatrick Read."

"Whoop! Whoop! Whoop!" came from the audience.

Surely my family hadn't shouted out those noises and Walker was under a strict gag order. Perhaps one of the rednecks was on a healing path.

I walked toward Mrs. Terry, who smiled broadly, the way she'd smiled whenever I entered her office with one of my schemes for administrative reform. Just as I reached her, I switched the mint to my left hand. I would save my rebellion for a more useful moment. She held my hand respectfully and looked into my eyes. Then she moved toward my ear and said, "You fly out of here, young man."

I was glad I'd ditched the mint.

When I got back to my seat, I was struck with the inevitable sentiment that comes anytime a high school band plays "Pomp and Circumstance" in fourteen different tempos.

The girls next to me, whom I'd never met before despite the fact that there were only a hundred people in our graduating class, were both crying. I was too. We held hands.

I'd made it. I hadn't been killed on the way. My parents hadn't thrown me out.

I listened to friends make speeches about bridges and futures and forks in the road. I was ready to puke from all the symbolism—the crossed rivers, the roads less traveled, the flight from the nest.

Graduation, I kept telling myself, was but a polite formality. I'd left this place years ago. I looked around at my fellow graduates. We knew each other in ways I would write about someday, hopefully with more kindness than I could have mustered at the time. In my mind I was already in New York. I was in Walker's arms. I was at the back of a dark theater, making tactless notes about actors who mangled my lines. I had shown up at the ceremony, but I was floating, somewhere near the rafters, wondering what my peers would do with the freedom that already coaxed, slapped, and soothed me.

I was gone, and gone was home.

The girls elbowed me to move the tassel of my mortarboard from right to left. Or left to right—who can remember? The processional music started, again in fourteen different tempos, and everyone tossed their caps into the air.

I stood on my chair and pointed at my family, the three voices that filled my head most often. The Colonel was madly snapping photos. Mom was crying so hard she had to gasp for breath. I snickered at Walker, as if to say, "Isn't this corny?" I could tell he got it, because he grinned, the way he did when I was being incorrigible.

The floor was full of screaming graduates, pogo-hopping all around me. Their polyester gowns filled up with air as they returned to the ground. I took a deep breath and aimed my mortarboard at my family. I cocked the cap back, knowing it would spin, sink, then flip-flop to the floor.

Mom reached out her hands to catch it.

I let go.

epilogue

"My mother helped me."

That's how I sum up my coming-out to new acquaintances. To this day, no one has replied "Me, too."

I was blessed to have indulgent parents—parents who allowed me to pursue creative impulses and relationships that must have frightened them; parents who encouraged me to take risks and make boldfaced mistakes; parents who, at key moments, had the good sense to look the other way. As the child of older parents, the cub of exhausted lions, I benefitted from the errors they'd made raising their older children. By the time they got around to me, they'd realized that unconditional love is less work than discipline.

My accounts of Mom's early support have been greeted by many as the stuff of unfathomable eccentricity, but it seems completely reasonable to me that parents address sexual identity around the time that they explain the mysteries of shaving and menstruation, when their children are just beginning to be motivated by hormones and curiosity.

At an early age, kids are asked to comprehend that God knowingly sent his virgin-born son to be crucified. However, a pair of boys or girls holding hands is somehow too much for their little brains to handle. That logic boggles the mind. Providing a non-judgmental space for kids to question their sexuality is just good parenting. It's not as if my mother *told* me to be gay. She just told me to be honest.

My father died of a brain tumor on Thanksgiving Day my first year at college. Walker had spent hours holding his hand and listening to his stories. I wish I'd talked with Dad about my relationship with Walker. In many ways, he gave his blessing without words. When someone is that sick, so much is transmitted through long stares and occasional hand squeezes. The Colonel knew.

I'm acutely aware of how easy I had it. Older gay folks remind me of this constantly, similar to the way parents tell their children "back in my day, we used to walk to school through ten feet of snow." For many generations of gay people, ten feet of snow is an apt analogy.

While countless young people are still trudging through ten feet of snow, without the support of family, friends, clergy, or teachers, my story is atypical. I got through high school without the all-too common horrors of many LGBT young people—the hiding, the violence, the suicide attempts. The name-calling and bullying I experienced were minor compared to what many kids face. I was lucky, but what a sad measure of fortune.

It could be that bland aesthetics spared me from considerable harm. The fact that I dressed in standard-issue tee shirts and jeans meant that I blended in while Jesse Fowler endured routine abuse. Ultimately, his wardrobe was an even bigger threat to the boys in the hallway than my having a boyfriend. Jesse wound up in New York, hanging out with the likes of Boy George and doing celebrity hair. He says that after years of feeling like he was wearing a strobe light on his head, New Yorkers make him feel conservative. (He says he wants to do my hair, which would figure, since I still get eight-dollar haircuts from men who tell fishing stories over the din of televised NASCAR races.)

Gay people certainly don't own the patent on teenage angst, and few people escape high school unscathed. I've met hundreds of people, straight and queer alike, with stories of their high school years—some funny, some inspiring, some downright terrifying. Even the most glamorous celebrities turn up on talk shows, fessing up to being tormented in some grisly fashion, often as the hosts unearth photos of them as lanky, buck-toothed dorks with bulging eyes. Freakishness is an equal opportunity affliction.

Ten years after graduating from high school, the world still seems like a neon-lit menagerie of jocks, preps, geeks, stoners, and cheerleaders to me. When I meet someone, I figure out which clique they were from and deal with them accordingly. Graduation doesn't break that world apart, it just scatters the participants. The trick is navigating that world in a way that preserves both one's voice and one's safety.

One of the ways I found safety was by living in urban gay communities where I could adopt people as surrogate family. Some of the members of my biological family raised religious objections to what they termed the "lifestyle" I'd "chosen." Rather than undertake the long-term and arduous process of understanding one another, I found a new family and spent the bulk of my twenties estranged from some of my blood siblings.

I know now that I didn't give my real family a chance because it was too painful to feel their disapproval. In some cases, I saw prejudice where it didn't exist and sometimes underestimated their capacity for love. I missed out on being a brother to them and an uncle to their children. Eventually, I stopped sending change-of-address cards when I moved and disappeared into my new family.

My chosen family had no learning curve with regard to sexuality because they were themselves gay. I didn't have to teach Gay 101 every time we spoke, as I had to with my real family. I didn't have to make apologies for being an activist. My new family was proud of me and never once issued the qualifier "but we don't approve of your lifestyle." LGBT folks are raised by people who mostly lack this kind of empathy. We're raised, all too often, by wolves.

Gradually, I'm reestablishing bonds with my blood siblings and other family members. I no longer view their acceptance as the determining factor in whether we can have a relationship, any more than I have to share their religious convictions. But I want to be in their lives.

Cultural shifts of the past decade have helped to demystify homosexuality for many, and I'm less of an obnoxious brat these days, both of which are conducive to healing conversation. Coming out was in many ways the easy part. Going home is considerably more daunting.

A good number of my high school classmates will grow old in Rockbridge County. Some have never left. When I go home to visit, I find some of them warming barstools, baiting the barmaid with familiar taunts. The boys I passed on my way to the cafeteria don't call me faggot anymore and I've long since retired my hillbilly voodoo dolls.

When I go home, we buy each other conciliatory pitchers of beer. They shake my hand too hard and ask me to tell exotic stories of life beyond the county line. Some of them have children. Some of them already have gay children, whether they know it yet or not. I ask them what it was like to win the state championship, with all those people screaming, all those years ago. They ask me what it was like to walk the halls alone, with all those people screaming, all those years ago. Now that we've outgrown *redneck* and *faggot*, we call each other by name.

acknowledgments

I'd like to thank the teachers who made high school safer: Susan Baker, Chris Bowring, Nikki Carr, Carter Drake, Yvonne Emerson, Rusty Ford, Lynda Gray, Peggy Hays, Julie Larsen, Nancy Leonhard, Wanda Leadbetter, Molly Pellicciaro, Carol Phemister, Deborah Pruett, and Kerrington Tillery.

Thanks also to those who have nurtured my writing: Randy Strawderman, most of all; my friends at the Shenandoah International Playwrights Retreat; Kimberly Krapf-Tetlow and Cynde Liffick from Studio Theatre of Richmond; Alicia Herr, Lee Hanson, Kathleen Vickery, Rosemary Doud, Ravigo Zomana, Don Davis, Erik Swallow and Thomas Long of *Our Own Community Press*; the Norfolk Gay Men's Book Group; the St. James Infirmary; Mark Beyer, Matt Brown, and Eric Rofes of the Gay Men's Health Summit collective; Window Media Editorial Director Chris Crain; the Radical Faeries; the Billy Club; Rex Mitchell at Phoenix Rising bookstores, who encouraged me to self-publish when I was twenty-one and gave me an evening every month for two years to perform new material.

My thanks go to Jim Alderson, Jim Baxter, Shelley Bindon, Jim Breeden, Angela Ciandro, Michael Collins, Bill Cooper, Delia Decourcy, Michael de Haas, Gavin Dillard, the Dick/Letcher family, Dhami Boo, Richard Dworkin, Darrel Farris, Karin Ferebee, John Frick, Phil Gates, Rick Gerharter, Patrick Giles, Hank Gold, Mark Griffin, Doug Grissom, Earl Grist, David Groff, Bill Harris,

Chris Hartless, Keltie Hays, Paul Hildebrand, Tim Hulsey, Jeff Johnson, Laura Joyner, Ernie Kidd, Jon Klein, Joseph Kramer, Whitney Larsen, Seth Leeper, Lyle, David Mariner, Mike, Bruce Mirken, Eddie Moreno, Tom Morke, Bob Mottley, my big sister Asa Dean Noble, Adam Olenn, Ian Philips (who listened patiently while I read each chapter over the phone), Tom Raisbeck, Julie Read, Rink Foto, Stuart Sanders, Stewart Scofield, Paul Selig, Martin Severino, Daddy Bob Smith, Reid Spice, Brad Stengel, Greg Taylor, Patti Tihey, Greg Tomso, Tim Updike, Ian Young, Jeff Walsh, Mark Weigle, Gweneth West, Michael Wheeler, and Jennifer Wise.

Thanks also to the good folks at Hill Street Press—my generous and whip-smart editor Patrick Allen; Anne Richmond Boston; Gabriel Wilmoth; and Tom Payton, who pushed me to write this book even though it scared the hell out of me.

To my overextended family—especially Mom—I love every damn one of you.